BECAUSE THEY WERE WOMEN

Because They Were Women

The Montreal Massacre

Library and Archives Canada Cataloguing in Publication

Title: Because they were women : the Montreal Massacre / Josée Boileau ;
    translated by Chantal Bilodeau.
Other titles: Ce jour-là. English
Names: Boileau, Josée, 1962- author. | Bilodeau, Chantal, 1968- translator.
Description: Series statement: A Feminist History Society book | Translation of:
    Ce jour-là.
Identifiers: Canadiana (print) 2020021165X | Canadiana (ebook) 20200211668 |
    ISBN 9781772601428 (softcover) | ISBN 9781772601435 (HTML)
Subjects: CSH: Montréal École Polytechnique Women Students Massacre, Montréal,
    Québec, 1989. | LCSH: Mass murder—Québec (Province)—Montréal.
Classification: LCC HV6535.C33 M65 2020 | DDC 364.152/340971428—dc23

Original title: Ce jour-là. Parce qu'elles étaient des femmes
Copyright © Les Éditions La Presse

Published under arrangement with Les Éditions La Presse, Montreal, QC, Canada

English-language translation copyright © 2020 Second Story Press

https://feministhistories.ca/

Original design by Simon L'Archevêque
Cover photo © Jacques Nadeau

Printed and bound in Canada

*Second Story Press gratefully acknowledges the support of the Ontario Arts Council and
the Canada Council for the Arts for our publishing program. We acknowledge the financial
support of the Government of Canada through the Canada Book Fund.*

Published by
Second Story Press
20 Maud Street, Suite 401
Toronto, ON M5V 2M5
www.secondstorypress.ca

A FEMINIST HISTORY SOCIETY BOOK

JOSÉE BOILEAU

Because They Were Women

The Montreal Massacre

DECEMBER 6, 1989

Translation by Chantal Bilodeau

Second Story Press

CONTENTS

Preface

Catherine Bergeron

MEMORY IS OFTEN SILENT, as if dozing off lulled by the warmth of a wood stove. But, every once in a while, it wants to talk. It wants to tell stories and histories. Because sooner or later, memory needs to be shared.

One day, there was the Comité Mémoire.

It was in 2014, the day after the ceremony marking the 25th anniversary of Montreal's École Polytechnique massacre. I remember someone said: "They can never be forgotten...." They. The fourteen young women killed because they were women.

That's when a handful of volunteers from diverse backgrounds coalesced into a committee. Ever since, every December 6, like a ritual, the Comité Mémoire holds a commemorative ceremony in collaboration with the City of Montreal, Polytechnique Montréal, and Moment Factory.

Memory is important. I find that it allows us to make the journey into the past and come back to the present with a bit more peace.

One day, there was the idea.

It would have been easy to mark the 30th anniversary of the Polytechnique massacre with more flowers, more speeches, more prayers, and more beams of light. "But why not [with] more soul?" suggested Jacques Duchesneau. That's how this book came into being.

I must thank this former chief of police for being the driving force behind this book. He was the first to imagine the portraits that would allow us to (re)discover what Anne-Marie Edward, Sonia Pelletier, Maryse Leclair, Barbara Daigneault, Maud Haviernick, Michèle Richard, Anne-Marie Lemay, Annie Turcotte, Hélène Colgan, Nathalie Croteau, Annie

St-Arneault, Maryse Laganière, Barbara Klucznik-Widajewicz, and my sister Geneviève Bergeron were and could have been.

I applaud his tenacity and his compassionate desire to paint the young women not just as victims, but also as people with habits, talents, loves, favorite sports, and dreams—all those human things that fill our ordinary and extraordinary days. I'll also let you in on a secret about my friend Jacques: it took him twenty years after the massacre to muster the strength to go back to Polytechnique. This book is a balm. For him as much as for me.

This book is also a necessity. It would have been unthinkable for it not to come into existence. It is a necessity because it locates December 6, 1989 within history and leaves a trace for future generations. It's a way to pass the torch. A way to pay tribute to the young women who have inspired so many people and who, from where they are now, urge us to carefully guard the place of women in society.

One day, there was the author.

You'll like Josée Boileau's words. No one but her could have taken us so expertly to the place where the personal and the historical meet. A journalist for over thirty years, who has worked for some of the most important media in Quebec—including as a columnist and editor-in-chief of *Le Devoir*—Josée has shown that we don't need answers so much as we need to tell.

She wrote with an open heart, a transmitter of memories offering us the opportunity to dive right into the heart of the before and after Polytechnique. Her views on the event, on feminism, and on society call for a new awareness. As she makes abundantly clear, the first pages of this tragedy were written well before that fateful December 6, 1989.

I deeply admire Josée. Her portraits of the victims also say a lot about us.

One day, there was everyone else.

The Polytechnique tragedy split my life in two: before and after the death of my sister. Before and after my missing her. For the last thirty years, I have kept alive the memory of those who have left us as a way to tie these two pieces together. Many others have done the same—families and friends, and also people moved by the massacre. Death has this amazing power to bring communities together in solidarity.

"You'll stay; we'll never lose touch," we told them. We wanted to continue the conversation with the deceased. Now this book will ensure that this happens.

I want to thank the voluntary members of the Comité Mémoire for their efforts in bringing this literary project to fruition: Jacques Duchesneau, Michel Petit, Romain A. Gayet, Annie-Clara Gravel, Florence Scanvic, Jonathan Landry-Leclerc, and Martine Robert. Thank you also to André Tessier.

Instead of urging us to ask why these fourteen young women have gone, they tried to remind us why they came.

I give a warm hug to the families and relatives of the victims, who graciously agreed to be interviewed, who dug through their photos and revisited their memories to allow this book to exist and touch us. This visit to the past is such a gift to our society.

My thoughts also go to all the injured, to the paramedics, the police officers, and the personnel of Polytechnique who lived through "that day" and are forever linked to the memory of this book.

Good-bye, my fourteen friends.

And though you and I, dear readers, are not them, we are definitely made of them.

Carpe diem.

Catherine Bergeron
President, the Comité Mémoire

Foreword

HOW CAN WE, THIRTY YEARS LATER, convey the horror of that night of December 6, 1989? How can we describe the unimaginable?

Perhaps by standing at the corner of Queen Mary Road and Decelles Avenue, at the foot of the road that goes up the hill and leads, a kilometer later, to Montreal's École Polytechnique. Perhaps by remembering the extreme winter cold, those nights when we quite literally freeze. And by imagining entering the building that was then at that intersection, the famous Café Campus, a favorite spot of Université de Montréal students for generations.

That Wednesday, there's room to sit by the huge bay window. The evening is young. It's what? 5:30 p.m.? Everyone is enjoying a quiet moment, all the more cozy given the thick fog and freezing drizzle outside.

But suddenly, something draws the attention of the few people at the tables. They start saying: "Hey, look...." The servers waiting on them go to the window and lean forward, trying to understand what's happening through the dark. And all of a sudden, they see.

A human tide is coming down the hill. Young people. Dozens of them, hundreds. Running. In shoes and T-shirts, distraught. They pour into the café, talking about a tragedy that they can't quite explain—What? A gunman at Polytechnique? Only one thing is clear: they had to flee. They talk over each other, become confused, search for words.

These young people, inadequately dressed, emerging from the dark and cold, fleeing their school in a panic, don't realize that they are, themselves, a scream in the night. A tragedy just took place. On a level that's never been seen before.

"We had no idea what was going on, but we knew that something terrible, something beyond what we could imagine, had happened," says Kathleen Lévesque.

This is Lévesque's first-hand memory. She was a journalism student at Université de Montréal then and a waitress at Café Campus, a cooperative that hired students. Years have passed, but for this experienced reporter, who long worked for *Le Devoir* and is now with *La Presse*, the emotion remains as vivid as it was that night.

She doesn't need an act of imagination to see the scene again. She only has to close her eyes and it comes rushing back. The door of the Café Campus opening and closing, students hurrying in to warm themselves, both physically and emotionally. The lights being turned on, the music being turned off. Tears. Tension. So many people, so much disbelief, so much pain. "It was very, very crowded. We gave them drinks. All we could do was hold their fear and listen to them."[1]

The sense of powerlessness was overwhelming, she remembers. "It's hard to explain." And it's still upsetting to this day.

Then there was the shock of finally learning, first through word-of-mouth, and then on the radio the coordinators of the Café were listening to in their office, that the gunman was after women. Only women. In Quebec. In 1989.

Thirty years later, we have to climb the hill and make the journey in the opposite direction. To remember what was—the massacre that evening, but also Quebec at that time. To realize that once the shock and trauma had subsided, the event gave rise to necessary battles and debates.

To resurrect what no longer is but should have been—the real tragedy of Polytechnique: fourteen remarkable young women who fell, ripped from their lives. And to highlight the memory that a society without them still managed to keep alive.

1. Interview with Kathleen Lévesque, September 4, 2019 (my translation).

DECEMBER 6, 1989

That afternoon

DECEMBER 6, 1989 IS NOT an exceptional day. But neither is it such a normal day.

At Montreal's École Polytechnique, it's the end of the term. The students are frantic—group projects to turn in, presentations to make, exams to prepare.... Polytechnique buzzes with activity day and night. There are people everywhere, all the time.

Geneviève Bergeron is in the computer lab with her teammate, Marco, to troubleshoot technical problems related to the project they will present in class later.

Maryse Leclair and her boyfriend, Benoît, have arrived early. She wants to finalize her presentation for her afternoon class. He promised he would attend.

Nathalie Croteau, for her part, left her parents' house in Brossard one hundred percent confident. She may not have slept much but her presentation is ready, reflecting the efforts she put into it.

Anne-Marie Lemay has spent hours looking over her notes. It's so exhausting! She scribbles a few words on the bulletin board of the apartment she shares with her roommates: "Tomorrow is the last day of class...and the last day of my life. Wow, that sounds really depressing at 3:00 in the morning."[1] When she leaves for Polytechnique on December 6, docs she remember her note? In any case, she doesn't erase it.

Maybe because winter hit Quebec hard this year, Jean-François Larivée is feeling a weight on his shoulders. This morning, he drove his

1. Interview with Anne-Marie Lemay's parents, June 7, 2019 (my translation).

wife, Maryse Laganière, to her job. She couldn't drive her own car because the lock had been tampered with. He dropped her off in front of the student entrance but didn't leave right away, looking at her for a long time as she walked away. Why this sudden sadness?

Feeling her husband's eyes on her, Maryse turned around, seemed surprised to still see him there, then rushed into the school. Time to go to work![2]

On the administrative side, today is not an ordinary day either. In the afternoon, William Winegard, Minister of State (Science and Technology) in Brian Mulroney's government, will be announcing a new funding program for industry.

Louis Courville, Interim President of Polytechnique, will be welcoming the minister. Courville assumed his position last summer when former president Roland Doré stepped down to run for Chairman of the Board of Directors. His successor will be appointed by the end of January.

Doré is not at Polytechnique on this cold Wednesday. He's in Lyon with a number of academics, including Gilles Cloutier, President of Université de Montréal. Mayor Jean Doré, who will be chairing the twinning of Montreal and Lyon, leads the impressive Montreal delegation.

At Polytechnique, the minister's presentation is very popular. Several professors and lecturers gather in the auditorium where Winegard gives his speech. Once the event is over, Courville goes back to his office accompanied by two members of the executive team and former Conservative party member Benoît Tremblay, who came with the minister. They need to discuss the financial and technical aspects of the funding program in order to determine the best way for Polytechnique to benefit from it.[3]

2. Correspondence with Jean-François Larivée, September 8, 2019.
3. Interview with Louis Courville, June 21, 2019.

At the Montreal Urban Community Police Service, the MUC Police[4] as it was then called, it's not an ordinary day either. In the late afternoon, several officers are sent to Saint-Léonard to gather clues to find the killer of a thirteen-year-old girl.

Valérie Dalpé's body was found a few weeks earlier, on October 19, in the Miron quarry dump. It was a gruesome murder, for which the police have no suspect. So, "in the evening of December 6, in the middle of a storm, forty detectives equipped with an elaborate questionnaire were […] going door-to-door showing photos of the young victim."[5]

It's not an ordinary day at all—but who could have known?—for a young man named Marc Lépine. He's twenty-five years-old, solitary, and marked by a difficult childhood and adolescence. He's the kind of person most would ignore or avoid, but he's not suspicious.

Throughout the day, he writes letters to his relatives, and one letter, not addressed to anyone in particular, that will soon reach all of Quebec.... He is mentally sound[6] and preparing to follow a precise plan hatched in advance.

His letters written—one of which he keeps on him—Lépine makes his way to Polytechnique. He's not a student, though he wishes he could be. Twice, his application was rejected because he didn't have good enough grades to be admitted to the prestigious school.

Nonetheless, he knows the place well, having visited it several times since his first application in 1986. And again, in early December, he was seen day after day, hanging out in a hallway, near the bookstore, at the cafeteria, and at the student co-op store....

4. The MUC Police is now called the City of Montreal Police Service. A list of acronyms and abbreviations can be found at the end of the book, p. 255.

5. André Cédilot, "Il y a trois ans, Valérie Dalpé était assassinée par un boucher" [Three years ago, Valérie Dalpé was assassinated by a butcher], *La Presse*, October 18, 1992 (my translation).

6. Blood alcohol, blood, and urine tests conducted by the Office of the Coroner after Lépine's death indicate that he didn't take any drugs or alcohol before the massacre. Teresa Z. Sourour, Office of the Coroner, Investigation reports, May 10, 1990, First part.

At 4:00 p.m. on the afternoon of December 6, he's in the Registrar's Office, where the doors are, as always, wide open. He sits and stretches his legs across the way. He's impossible to miss. "He's sitting on the bench at the entrance of the office, near the door and, because of his position, he's blocking access to the entrance. Indeed, he's sitting in a way that makes coming in difficult [...]. A number of times, he's seen rummaging through a green plastic bag, whose contents he seems to want to hide. He doesn't talk to anyone and no student addresses him. At one point, one of the employees working at the desk asks if she can help him. He doesn't answer and leaves."[7]

It's 4:40 p.m. In a few minutes, everything is going to change. This not-so-ordinary day will slip to the dark side of history.

7. Ibid, Second part, p. 6–7.

Those 20 minutes[1]

AFTER MARC LÉPINE WALKS AWAY from the Registrar's Office, he goes up to the third floor. At 4:45 p.m., he's leaning against the wall in a hallway still holding the green plastic bag, which visibly contains a long object.

Meanwhile, on the second floor, the line in the server room is getting longer. "Everyone has laptops now, but in those days, we had one central computer with monitors throughout the school, and all of these things connected to the server room on the second floor. Students would come in to pick up reports or drawings…," explains Guy Brunelle, who was working that night along with a colleague.[2]

Not far from there, in classroom C-230.4, sixty students have been in class since 3:00 p.m. One by one, the small groups present their work in front of the class, under the supervision of Yvon Bouchard, Professor of Mechanical Engineering, and Adrian Cernea, Professor of Electrical Engineering. Finally, it's 5:00 p.m., the last hour of the last class of the semester!

That's when Lépine makes his way back to the second floor. A few minutes before 5:10 p.m., he takes the hallway that leads to C-230.4, an isolated classroom. There's no reason to take this hallway other than to go to that room.

Which is precisely where Lépine is going.

---

1. Details about the sequence of events of the Polytechnique massacre vary among news stories, documentaries, and testimonials. For this book, we essentially rely on Coroner Teresa Z. Sourour's report from May 10, 1990. When different sources are used, they are indicated.
2. Interview with Guy Brunelle, June 19, 2019 (my translation).

He enters the classroom at 5:10 p.m., and goes straight to the student who is presenting.

"Lépine is holding a rifle with both hands [...] and he says: 'All right everyone, stop everything!' He abruptly shoots towards the ceiling and says: 'Girls to the left and guys to the right.' [...] No one reacts to his order. He repeats the same thing in a more forceful tone. [...] Once the groups have split, he says: 'OK, guys get out, girls, stay here.'"[3]

The men exit in utter confusion, but not fast enough for Lépine. "Move your asses!" he yells—and that probably contributes to some of them feeling that this is a new end-of-the-semester joke. This guy must have shot a blank. In fact, isn't he smiling?

Students and professors pick up the pace, not imagining for a second what's going to happen next.

The nine women in the group have been sent to the back of the classroom, far from the door, far from any possibility of escape. Lépine moves in closer.

France Chrétien, who survived the massacre, remembers: "Once all the guys were out, there was a moment's silence when no one said anything. Then Lépine asked: 'Are you wondering why you're here?' Annie St-Arneault shot back: 'Who are you?'"[4]

Who is he? He's a man who's against feminists, against women like them, he replies. No, says Nathalie Provost: "We're not feminists, we're girls who like science!"[5]

There are a few variations of this exchange, which is etched into people's memories. Nathalie herself recounted it this way when she talked to journalists from her hospital bed two days after the shooting: "I told him we were just women studying engineering—we were not necessarily feminists."[6] In Coroner Sourour's report, the answer becomes: "We're not feminists—we've never fought against men."[7]

3. Teresa Z. Sourour, Office of the Coroner, Investigation reports, May 10, 1990, Second part, p. 7 (my translation).

4. Interview with France Chrétien, July 25, 2019 (my translation).

5. Ibid.

6. Paul Roy, "Il y a un seul coupable et il est mort" [There's only one culprit and he's dead], La Presse, December 9, 1989 (my translation).

7. Teresa Z. Sourour, Office of the Coroner, op. cit.

But finding the exact words is irrelevant since Lépine has no intention of listening to them. He starts to shoot, unloading a round of bullets on the small group.

"The rest is sort of in slow motion in my head," says France today. "I threw myself on the ground and turned around. At times I could hear everything; at other times it was just noise." Other women—one? several?—fall on top of her.

And then this: "It was like it was raining. It was raining bits of concrete everywhere."[8]

Josée Martin, another student in the group, will tell *La Presse* on the first anniversary of the massacre that she had time to crouch down. A bullet hit her in the arm. "That's when I realized that he wasn't shooting blanks. I couldn't believe it. No one could believe it."[9]

Lépine empties an entire magazine in C-230.4: a total of thirty bullets.

"Lépine," she continues, "had a smile on his face. He seemed very proud of himself. It's as if he was in a dream and everything was going according to plan. He left the classroom without so much as a glance. He was probably thinking about his next victims."[10]

He leaves behind him nine collapsed students. Three are seriously injured: Josée Martin, Nathalie Provost, and France Chrétien. Their six classmates—Hélène Colgan, Nathalie Croteau, Barbara Daigneault, Anne-Marie Lemay, Sonia Pelletier, and Annie St-Arneault—will never get up again.

The gunman next takes the hallway that leads to the photocopiers in C-229. There, he shoots again, injuring first a man and a woman, then another woman he bumps into as he's approaching the first two people.

8. France Chrétien, op. cit.

9. Suzanne Colpron, "Je pense toujours qu'un malade va me tirer" [I always think a crazy man is going to shoot me], *La Presse*, December 1, 1990 (my translation).

10. Ibid.

He backtracks and goes to C-228, which communicates with the server room. A class is in session. Lépine stays at the door. "He looks at everyone and aims at a student in the back of the class. He tries to shoot her twice but his rifle refuses to work."[11]

He turns on his heels and goes to the emergency stairway just a few steps away.

In the server room, Brunelle and his colleague, Huguette, hear strange sounds. But the computers around them are so loud that they don't pay attention. That is, until a student rushes in announcing that there's a shooter in the school....

Brunelle barely has time to digest this information when something grabs his attention. He says: "I saw a woman in the distance, hiding her face behind a sheet of paper to protect herself. I realized it was serious." The lecturer from the class next door comes in, "white as a ghost," and tells them that a guy carrying a rifle showed up, aiming to shoot, but it didn't work.

"I made all the students come to my side," says Brunelle. One of them has the reflex to first lock the door that opens to the hallway, the one in front of which Lépine was standing a moment ago. A "brilliant idea,"[12] says Brunelle, thirty years later.

Once in the emergency stairway, Lépine doesn't go anywhere; he simply checks the functioning of his rifle. A student walks by and hears him say: "Shit! I'm out of bullets!" The student doesn't pay much attention and continues on his way.

Once he gets to the photocopiers, however, the student sees the three injured people on the ground. What he just heard in the stairway suddenly becomes clear. He turns around. Lépine is reloading his rifle. He lifts it. The student flees towards the escalator that leads to the cafeteria. He hears the gunshot from there.

Lépine goes back to C-228 but this time, the door is locked—he can't get in. So he shoots at the door.

"He kept shooting, he wouldn't stop!" remembers Brunelle. "I was afraid if he made it through the door, he would come over to our side. That's when it occurred to me to make everyone crawl under the false floor."

11. Teresa Z. Sourour, op. cit., p. 8.
12. Guy Brunelle, op. cit.

Back then, he explains, computer cords ran under the floor of the huge room, in a space about eighteen inches deep. The cords took up a lot of space, but it was still possible to crawl in, which is what he, along with his colleague Huguette, the lecturer, and the eight or nine male students in the room, set out to do. "In such circumstances, you manage to squeeze in!" exclaims Brunelle.

"But before, I gave two or three magnetic tapes to the guys—that's what we were using back then—and I told them that if he came in, we'd throw them at him. It might slow him down."

Luckily, the door holds and Lépine walks away. Once again, he takes the hallway where the three injured students are. He bumps into a woman who is coming up the escalator, on her way to the server room. He shoots, and hits her. But she manages to get up, run to the emergency stairway, and seek refuge on the fifth floor.

Lépine doesn't follow her. He goes towards a counter, on which he leans to reload his rifle. A young woman is hiding underneath. He sees her and shoots. Once. Twice. But he misses.

Under the false floor of the server room, everyone is silent. From there, they can clearly hear the gunshots. "Dozens and dozens of them…. We kept hearing them and wondering where he was,"[13] recounts Brunelle.

The gunman continues on his deadly journey, begun less than fifteen minutes earlier. He arrives near the offices of Financial Services.

However, the news that a massacre is underway has started to spread throughout the building and Financial Services were just informed through a phone call. Employees have to take cover.

Maryse Laganière was about to leave—she had already put on her boots and her corduroy jacket. She rushes to the door of her office, room B-218, to lock it. Lépine is nearby. He sees her maneuver. He "runs back to prevent her from locking [it]."[14] They fight, on opposite sides of the door, to control the handle, whose latch, when it's pushed in, automatically locks the door.

13. Ibid.
14. Teresa Z. Sourour, Office of the Coroner, op. cit., 9.

Maryse finally succeeds. But there's a narrow window next to the door. Lépine sees the young woman back away. He shoots through the window. Maryse is hit. Her wound will prove fatal.

The gunman hurries back to the escalator. On the landing of the second floor, he handles his weapon, then goes down one floor. "It's now 5:20 p.m."[15]

– ※ –

On the main floor, Lépine goes to the cafeteria. About a hundred people are there and some have heard that something really worrisome happened on the second floor. A sick joker, a thief, a crazy shooter? The noise and confusion are such that the manager is evacuating people through the service door.

But Lépine has found his way in and is aiming at a young woman near the kitchen. Barbara-Maria Klucznik-Widajewicz falls under the bullets.

Panic sets in; everyone tries to run away. Lépine moves slowly, firing a few more shots. Someone else is injured.

At the other end of the cafeteria, he finds the Poly-Party room, an open storage space where wood panels and large speakers have been stored. Geneviève Bergeron and Anne-Marie Edward have found refuge there. But Lépine has spotted them. He approaches and shoots. Death, again.

Next, he sees two students hiding under a table: a man and a woman. He orders them to come out. They obey—but he doesn't shoot. Instead, he leaves the cafeteria, takes the hallway that leads to the stationery store, and goes back to the second floor where his first victims are.

He uses the escalator, which is now still—someone had the presence of mind to stop it to slow him down. When he gets to the third floor, there are still several people there. He shoots, injuring two young men and a young woman.

"Lépine then takes a narrow hallway and after turning left, ends up fifteen feet farther in classroom B-311. It's about 5:25 p.m."[16]

15. Ibid.
16. Ibid. 10.

– ☀ –

In B-311, no one knows what just happened on the two floors below. They're all busy listening to student presentations, as part of Professor Jean-Paul Baïlon's course, Mechanical and Thermal Characterization of Materials.[17] Three students are already on stage, among them Maryse Leclair, ready to present their final project.

Lépine barges into the classroom and approaches the stage. He tells the men to get out and immediately shoots Maryse. Then, he turns around and fires at students in the first rows.

A student yells, "Get down!" and several of them hit the floor. Others try to exit through the door in the back. Maud Haviernick is among them, but Lépine sees her and aims, hitting her with several fatal shots. The young woman will later be found "in the hallway in front of the door."[18]

While Lépine's attention is focused on the back of the room, some students rush towards the door at the front. Michèle Richard is following her boyfriend, who wants to sound the alarm and get help. But Lépine spots her. He kills her with a single shot.

He next shifts his attention to the students and professor lying on the ground between the long tables that fill the width of the room. Trying to hide from him, they can't see what's going on, but they can follow his footsteps, and they can most of all hear him.

Lépine paces the room, bends down to see who is under the tables, and aims at four young women, one after the other. He kills Annie Turcotte and injures three others. But he ignores a woman with very short hair.

He changes his magazine and climbs on a table in the back of the room. Walking from table to table, he makes his way to the front while continuing to shoot. He steps on stage where Maryse is lying. Severely injured, she's moaning and asking for help. He stabs her three times. She will be his last victim.

But it's not over yet.

"He puts his knife, two boxes containing twenty bullets each, and his cap on the professor's desk. Then, he sits on the stage. He takes off his

17. Police report of Detective Sergeant Jean-Guy Dupuis, December 11, 1989.
18. Teresa Z. Sourour, Office of the Coroner, First part, op. cit.

jacket, wraps it around the barrel of his weapon and, after saying 'Oh shit!' he shoots himself in the head, using the last bullet in the magazine. Another box of twenty bullets is on a chair in the front of the classroom near the door."[19]

Now it's over.

It's not even 5:30 p.m.

19. Ibid, Second part, 10.

That evening

FOR EVERYONE LYING ON THE FLOOR of classroom B-311, Marc Lépine's suicide marks the end of the massacre. Professor Jean-Paul Baïlon slowly gets up and tells the students to leave through the door in the back of the room, as calmly as possible, and without looking at the stage.[1]

But he doesn't leave. He walks around the room, horrified to discover that four of his students, all women, are dead. Another is severely injured. He immediately tries to reassure her, then goes back and forth several times between the hallway and where the girl is, watching for help.

In the school, no one knows that the shooter is dead. Fear keeps spreading as everyone becomes aware of the events, which happened at warp speed.

This is true for Yin Fan. The young woman, recently arrived from China, came across Lépine on the landing of the third floor. He fired at her twice and hit her. But before she realized what had happened, another student, also injured, dragged her out of range of the shooter.

"I felt someone push me and I followed. We ran along a hallway and hid in one of the classrooms. Then we heard footsteps and another gunshot. And we waited."[2]

There are three of them hiding in the third-floor classroom located near B-311. Yin doesn't speak fluent French, which exacerbates her feelings of helplessness. What's happening?

In C-230.4, the first classroom where Lépine opened fire, Josée Martin, France Chrétien, and Nathalie Provost haven't moved. "We heard

1. Report of Detective Sergeant Yves Brien, December 7, 1989.
2. Interview with Yin Fan, August 2, 2019 (my translation).

so many gunshots coming from all over that we thought there were several shooters,"[3] remembers France.

After several long minutes, the women get up, unaware of their injuries. As they look around, they realize that their classmates are no longer alive. Nathalie tries to go get help, but she's too badly hurt to make it to the door. However, she thinks she sees Lépine: "He's coming back!" she yells. For the three students, this is pure hell.

A few minutes later, someone comes in. In fact, two people do but they're not shooters; they're panicked students looking for an emergency exit. They don't even seem to notice the women. Two more students follow— men worried about the women they had to leave behind when they were told to get out of the classroom. When they see the state their classmates are in, they hurry to get help.

France finally manages to get out of the room. She comes across other injured students lying near the photocopiers. Then, she says, "someone grabbed me and took me to a kind of bookstore in the back. There, they told me I was bleeding. That's how I realized I was hurt."[4] But no police officer or paramedic is there to help. She can only rely on the people already present, who are reeling from the shock of what just happened.

Louis Courville is in his office when he's told that a tragedy is unfolding in his institution. A student barges in, shaking, locks the door behind him, and announces that a crazy man is shooting people in the school. At the same time, they hear gunshots. They don't know it yet but those are the shots that killed Maryse Laganière.

Courville tries to dial 911 but he can't get a line. So many people are calling for help that the lines are all busy. This is made worse by the fact that several public phones of this pre-cellular era are being repaired.

Meanwhile the gunshots continue, in such a way that it's easy to believe there are several shooters, says Courville.[5] "Through the window I could see hundreds of students, in their shirts, pour out the doors and jump over the snowbanks,"[6] he adds.

3. Interview with France Chrétien, July 25, 2019 (my translation).
4. Ibid.
5. Isabelle Paré, "La peur de l'oubli" [The fear of oblivion], Le Devoir, December 6, 2014.
6. Ibid.

– ✳ –

In May 1990, a report about the tragedy is published. Coroner Teresa Z. Sourour, who is also a pathologist, begins by presenting the autopsies of the gunman and the fourteen victims, noting that given the severity of their injuries, none of the young women could have survived. The second part of her report details the sequence of events, which provides an explanation for why the wait seemed so long to people who were at Polytechnique that night.

The 911 call center in Montreal receives the first call for help at 5:12:28 p.m. It comes from a Polytechnique student and lasts a little over two minutes. The report states: "The student locates the shooting on the second floor. He explains that the individual fired once, asked the men to get out, and kept the women. Then, he adds that the individual is shooting everywhere. During the call, the operator can hear gunshots as well as someone moaning. Throughout the conversation, the operator [of the 911 call center] tries to forward information to the police dispatch center. He encounters difficulties and can't transfer the call."[7]

This communication problem is due to a new procedure being implemented. The 911 call center receives all calls requiring an emergency response and routes them to the appropriate department. The center is located in the room right next to the MUC Police dispatch center but a few weeks ago, operators had to start forwarding information through the computer instead of through written notes, which is what they had always done. The new procedure is not quite working yet....

911 receives a second call. It comes from a Polytechnique security guard who was alerted by a professor that "an armed individual is harassing students in C-230.4."[8] This call is transferred to Urgences-santé, who say they have been informed and have dispatched ambulances to the location.

However, 911 doesn't know the exact address of Polytechnique on the vast Université de Montréal campus. Working with a new computerized routing system implemented only a few days ago, the center doesn't have the address in its database and will systematically ask everyone calling from

7. Teresa Z. Sourour, Office of the Coroner, Investigation reports, May 10, 1990, Second part, 15–16 (my translation).
8. Ibid. 42.

Polytechnique for it. This slows down the forwarding of the information to Urgences-santé paramedics.

The calls keep coming in with, always, moaning and gunshots in the background. Once again, there's confusion in the routing of the calls to the police department. Finally, at 5:15:58 p.m., the police are alerted about the incident. Three minutes and thirty seconds have gone by since the first call. A delay far too long, indicates Coroner Sourour in her report.

Two minutes later, at 5:17:58 p.m., police cruisers from District 31 are alerted that a serious incident has taken place at the university. But the incident is given the code of a hostage taking. It is specified that a suspect armed with a rifle is holding twenty women hostages in a classroom on the second floor and that he fired in the air. All of this is happening at 2500 Edouard Montpetit Boulevard, the dispatcher adds incorrectly, without specifying that the location is Polytechnique.

Based on this information, the police operation gets underway. Two cruisers hurry...to the student housing tower on Edouard Montpetit Boulevard. It's 5:19 p.m.

A correction is made over the radio a few seconds later: it's up there, on the hill, at Polytechnique that the tragedy is happening! The cruisers change direction. At 5:21 p.m., they're finally at the right place.

A first ambulance arrives. Others soon follow. Injured students immediately approach the paramedics to receive first aid treatment, and to alert them that there are people in pretty bad shape inside who need their help.

Yet no one goes in....

Police officers, now in greater numbers, are responding to a hostage situation. They start by establishing a security perimeter around the school, "hundreds of meters away from the building."[9] It's forbidden to go inside.

Already, there are serious communication problems with the police dispatch center, and a lack of coordination between police officers. On top of that, Urgences-santé is not kept informed of the status of the situation. Not knowing the scope of the event, they have a difficult time determining the number of personnel to send to Polytechnique.

It's almost 5:25 p.m. when a student call is transferred directly to the police. The student mentions gunshots and injuries. One minute later,

9. Ibid. 19.

another student inside the school is heard over the radio. He describes the gunman in detail.

Another call. The person on the line suggests pulling the fire alarm. Permission is granted. Someone else thinks it's a bad idea because firefighters will rush to the school even though they're not needed. Too late, the alarm is already blaring, adding to the confusion in the building. It's 5:27 p.m. Eight firetrucks eventually show up.

Calls reporting gunshots, and dead and injured people, keep coming in, so some police officers suggest going in. Those in charge think it's better to wait for additional officers, including the tactical unit, in order to show up in strength. A decision is also made to call back the officers from the Crimes Against Persons section who were sent to Saint-Léonard to investigate the murder of young Valérie Dalpé.

In short, everyone is waiting. Coroner Sourour summarizes the situation this way: "In that moment, no intervention strategy is underway, nor is there a strategy about to be implemented or even formulated."[10]

The same confusion and the same wait directive prevent first responders from providing assistance to the injured inside the school. So, a young man already in the building takes it upon himself to lend a hand. He's a student at Polytechnique, but he also works as a paramedic. He's there because he had classes that day.

He goes from person to person, trying to care for everyone. When his paramedic colleagues finally enter the building, he stays to help.

At 5:36 p.m., a crucial piece of information arrives: the suspect has committed suicide. Finally, police officers are authorized to go in and check the building. Baïlon quickly intercepts them and asks that they follow him to classroom B-311, where Lépine shot himself.

10. Ibid. 52 (my translation).

Five minutes later, at 5:41 p.m., "the medical emergency team receives authorization to enter the building accompanied by the police."[11] They go in at 5:45 p.m., even though they have been outside since 5:24 p.m.

They're told to go to the second and third floors, where many injured students have been found. But the confusion is such that, once inside, paramedics have no one to guide them through the labyrinth of hallways. As a result, they miss the cafeteria and have a hard time finding their way once they get to the third floor. Armed undercover police officers add to the confusion. Are they accomplices of the gunman?

In addition, "because of a lack of adequate equipment, paramedics are unable to communicate with one another or with other resources outside the building, which makes their work that much more difficult."[12]

On the police side, most of the officers continue to maintain a security perimeter around the school. Inside the building, police work to protect the crime scenes. No one can get in, not even relatives. Not even people who are desperate, like Jean-François Larivée, Maryse Laganière's husband, who came to pick her up after work. Even after badgering the police, there's no way to get any information. Larivée tries everything to make his way into the building, then runs from one stretcher to another to try to find his wife. To no avail.

The situation is completely unheard of for the MUC Police. It's also complex to manage. Jacques Duchesneau, then Director of the Organized Crime section and second-in-command during hostage situations—and one of the first to arrive on the scene because he was coming out of a class at Université de Montréal—later explained it this way: "There's screaming, victims are being carried out, dead bodies are found, there's blood everywhere. People in a panic come running out. Maybe the suspect is among them."[13]

"I was scared," Carole Bilodeau, a former nurse who had become a police officer two years earlier will recount. She's among the first officers to go inside the school. "We didn't know if the shooter was really dead; we

11. Ibid. 20.

12. Ibid. 28–29 (my translation).

13. Michèle Ouimet, "Polytechnique vue de l'intérieur, 20 ans après" [Polytechnique seen from the inside, 20 years later], La Presse, November 30, 2009 (my translation).

didn't know if he would suddenly show up behind us; we had no idea what could happen."[14]

One last thing needs to happen, and it will take hours. The police and the security staff of Polytechnique search the entire building. About a hundred officers check some 450 classrooms.

That's how the police are able to conclude that Lépine, whose identity will be confirmed the morning of December 7, acted alone.

This search also allows everyone who was still hiding to come out.

That's the case for the small group who crawled under the false floor in the server room. "We stayed there for about forty minutes," remembers Brunelle. "At one point, the shots stopped. Then, through the PA system, someone told us to evacuate the school slowly, walking not running. We came out of the hole. It was crazy! There was so much blood on the second floor that it was hard to make our way out. And we saw so many injured...."[15]

The people hiding in the kitchen of the cafeteria leave through the emergency exit. They don't see anything. They don't even know what happened.

It takes until 6:02 p.m. for the first severely injured victim to be evacuated. By 6:41 p.m., every victim has been transported to a hospital.

Some are in shock, like Yin Fan, who says that despite her injuries, she didn't want to go to the hospital. She kept saying: "I can't go, I have an exam tomorrow!" Baïlon, who had found her in the classroom where she had been hiding with two other students, has to reassure her: there's no need to worry about the exam. She finally agrees to let first responders take charge of her. She will be hospitalized for weeks and undergo several operations.[16]

Another injured student, Asmaa Mansour, spends long minutes alone, lying on the ground on the second floor, in pain and disoriented by the blaring alarm. A student finally administers first aid, using his sweater to make

14. Interview with Carole Bilodeau, June 12, 2019 (my translation).
15. Interview with Guy Brunelle, June 19, 2019 (my translation).
16. Op. cit.

a tourniquet. Another man in a suit, who doesn't identify himself, holds the young woman's arm at a precise angle to ease her pain. He stays with her until help arrives. "He was crying, and I kept screaming: 'Help me, I'm going to die.'"[17]

Thirty years later, Asmaa remembers the two paramedics who took care of her and something one of them said, which comforted her, and she never forgot: "In the ambulance, I said: 'I'm going to die, right?' And one of the paramedics said: 'No, I won't let you die. You're too beautiful to die....'"[18]

Maryse Laganière is also injured but she doesn't survive.

To get to her, the door, which she locked when Lépine was coming at her, has to be forced open. Once that's done, police officer Carole Bilodeau stays by her side. "Maryse was lying on the ground, unconscious. She was severely injured. I talked to her, but she didn't react. I took her pulse, I waited for help.... It was crazy, we couldn't send radio messages out, they kept coming in! I held her arm and stayed with her until she passed. It didn't take very long...."[19]

Realizing that death hit in a place where we would never expect such a tragedy is upsetting for the officer, and for so many people that night.

France recounts that once the paramedics entered the school, they started with the people who were the worst off. She was waiting for her turn: "Finally, a man said: 'I'll take you to the hospital, it'll be faster.'"[20] But France doesn't have her health insurance card, which she left with her personal belongings in classroom C-230.4. And she's determined to retrieve it. Exceptional circumstances often cause strange obsessions, she explains.

When the paramedics see her come into the classroom, they immediately take charge of her and refuse to let her go. At one point, she notices that a paramedic is going around the young women lying on the ground. "He said: 'I've checked them all.' Which meant: 'They're all dead.' That's when I realized.... Suddenly, it was real."[21]

17. Suzanne Colpron, "J'ai l'impression que je ne suis plus bonne à rien" [I feel like I've become useless], *La Presse*, December 1, 1990 (my translation).
18. Interview with Asmaa Mansour, July 5, 2019 (my translation).
19. Op. cit.
20. Op. cit.
21. Ibid.

The deceased women are all found as soon as the police enter Polytechnique...except for Geneviève Bergeron and Anne-Marie Edward, who hid in the back of the cafeteria. Their bodies will not be discovered until 7:15 p.m., when police officers are going around the school.

Courville is going around too, walking through the building transformed into a war zone: there are bullet holes all over the floors, the walls, and the ceilings. And all this blood....

He runs through a series of urgent tasks in his head. First, get the list of victims so their relatives can be contacted as soon as possible. To do that, he enlists his own family—he sends his wife, Jeanne Dauphinais, to the different hospitals to find everyone. His daughter, who speaks Mandarin, will serve as an interpreter for Yin Fan when she gets to the hospital.

Courville also has to contact Roland Doré, the future Chair of the Board of Directors, who is in France. And he has to meet with the families of the victims, already waiting at the door of the building in greater and greater numbers....

In addition, he needs to find a classroom where the police can set up their headquarters, another that can serve as an infirmary, and a third one for journalists, who will hold a number of press conferences throughout the night.

And still another one—is this real?—that will serve as a makeshift morgue. That's where Coroner Paul G. Dionne's team will examine the fourteen victims before bringing the families to identify them.

The vice-rector of Université de Montréal, Pierre Robert, lends his help to Courville. Since the president is on that same trip to France, it falls on the vice-rector to make decisions that night. He asks Courville to direct people waiting for news of their relatives, in the cold and snow—it has started snowing—to the university's main pavilion, the one with the tower.

A small crowd takes the road that leads to the great tower. Courville is with them. There, wanting to reassure people as much as possible, he reads the list of victims and indicates to what hospital they have been taken. As soon as this information is shared, the room starts to empty.

Except there are names missing from the list—the names of the fourteen young women who are neither in the hospitals nor on the grounds of Polytechnique, where journalists are witnessing poignant reunions between worried families and students coming out of the school.

The relatives of the fourteen women wait in the main pavilion. Then, late into the night, they are invited to go back to Polytechnique. One after the other, they will make their way through the classroom turned into a morgue.

Once the victims have been taken charge of and the school has been evacuated, all the people who were at Polytechnique that night are released into the world. What else is there to do but tell your relatives that everything is fine and go home? There are no places to receive treatment for fear or emotional pain.

And to whom can this unimaginable event really be told? Few will confide right away, even to their relatives. This will come with time, sometimes after years of silence. Others will choose never to speak of that evening again. Out of a desire for privacy as much as out of pain.

Several witnesses will mention a sense of something being off with the rest of the world. When she takes the subway to go home in the early morning, after hours of horror during the events and at the makeshift morgue, Officer Bilodeau describes her feelings this way:

> It was unreal. The whole time I was at the school, I couldn't believe that something like that had happened. I had to see all the women to realize. Then, when I took the subway, I was shocked to see that people were living their lives as if nothing had happened.[22]

22. Op. cit.

–·✳·–

On December 7, 1989, the day after the tragedy, it's so cold outside that when people tried to "fly the flags of Polytechnique at half-mast, [...] the pulleys were stuck. The Montreal firefighters had to use their ladder to pry them loose."[23]

It's an apt symbol of the glacial hand that, since the previous night, has been keeping a tight grip on people's hearts.

23. Jean V. Dufresne, "Des roses dans la neige" [Roses in the snow], *Le Devoir*, December 8, 1989 (my translation).

QUEBEC, AT THAT TIME

Before, 1969–1989

THE BATTLES

MARC LÉPINE SAID IT to his victims, just like he wrote it in his letters on the day of the massacre: his target was "feminists who have ruined my life." From this unsettling statement, we have to remember that, in fact, whoever was, like him, born in Quebec in the 1960s, had seen their lives completely transformed by the formidable social upheaval that is feminism.

Throughout the entire Western world, youth from that decade are demanding an end to shackles and dreaming of peace and freedom. But the great movement that will take place at that time, and that still persists to this day, is women's fight for gender equality.

In Quebec, we only have to go back twenty years before the Polytechnique massacre to see how each year brought a surge of progress for women.

At the turn of the 20th century, feminists are focused on acquiring the right to vote—a right secured at the federal level since the 1921 elections, but still being denied in the Quebec elections. The battle is long; it won't be won until 1940. It will take even longer for Indigenous people, both men and women: in Quebec, they don't obtain the right to vote until 1969.

Voting is one thing, but it has to lead to the next step: being elected. It takes another twenty years to pass that hurdle. In 1961, Claire

Kirkland-Casgrain[1] becomes the first woman elected to the Legislative Assembly of Quebec. But she will remain the only woman for more than a decade....

Luckily, she cares deeply about women's issues. Soon appointed minister, in 1964 she passes legislation that gives married women legal autonomy. This means that women can now open a bank account or sign a lease without their husband's authorization.

This legislative change is important but it's still too timid for the new wave of militant feminists, who are bursting with energy during the 1960s. They see big—gender equality has to go beyond laws and translate into day-to-day life. And that begins with control over their own body, from access to contraception to the legalization of abortion.

In 1969, twenty years before the Polytechnique massacre, "the pill," as it's commonly known, finally becomes accessible as a contraceptive to all women in Canada. Approved since 1960, it was previously only prescribed to women diagnosed with "gynecological problems." In that same year of 1969, Dr. Henry Morgentaler opens his first clinic in Montreal where he performs abortions.

In addition, buoying the hopes of the late 1960s, the work of the Royal Commission on the Status of Women in Canada, known as the Bird Commission, marks a real turning point in the official recognition of feminism as a driving force.

1. This is how she was known as a politician. Later, she will go by the name of Marie-Claire Kirkland.

Claire Kirkland-Casgrain, the first woman minister appointed in the history of Quebec.

JOHN HUMPHREY
COMMISSIONER
COMMISSAIRE

MRS. LOLA M. LANGE
COMMISSIONER
COMMISSAIRE

MLLE JEANNE LAPOINTE
COMMISSIONER
COMMISSAIRE

MRS. JOHN BIRD
CHAIRMAN
PRÉSIDENTE

MRS. DORIS G. OGILVIE
COMMISSIONER
COMMISSAIRE

MISS ELSIE G. MᶜGILL
COMMISSIONER
COMMISSAIRE

Public hearings held by the Royal Commission on the Status of Women in Canada, chaired by Florence Bird (center), who is identified as "Mrs. John Bird" here.

Recommendations and actions

The Bird Commission is established in Ottawa in 1967 by the Liberal government of Lester B. Pearson, in response to pressures from women's organizations wanting gender discrimination to finally be acknowledged.

The Commission is chaired by a woman, Florence Bird—a first. Her executive secretary, Monique Bégin, a future minister in Pierre Elliott Trudeau's government, is a dynamic Québécoise. She encourages the commissioning of several studies that document different aspects of women's lives. Many women researchers from Quebec are involved—Marie-Andrée Bertrand, Alice Parizeau, Micheline Dumont. They will become influential intellectuals.

The Bird Commission is extremely popular. Over a period of six months, public hearings are held all over Canada and women turn up in massive numbers to speak out. Its report, published in December 1970, includes 167 recommendations: equal pay, maternity leave, the creation of daycare centers, alimony, access to abortion, access to leadership positions, solutions to specific problems faced by Indigenous women in relation to the Indian Act.... Everything is there.

Everything is also there on the militant front. In Quebec, it's an explosion!

First, new feminists organize. Their efforts range from the foundation, in 1966, of Fédération des femmes du Québec (FFQ)—a large coalition led by Thérèse Casgrain, a historic figure in the fight for women's right to vote in Quebec—to the creation of the decidedly radical Front de libération des femmes du Québec (Quebec women's liberation front) (FLF), active from 1969 to 1971.

Despite its brief existence, FLF will leave an indelible mark because of its spectacular actions—the most popular one actually leading to concrete results.

In March 1971, in the aftermath of the 1970 October Crisis, one of the members of FLF, Lise Balcer, is called to testify at the trial of Front de Libération du Québec (FLQ) member Paul Rose. She refuses. In those days, women couldn't serve as jurors; why would they be credible witnesses? She's found to be in contempt of court. On the day of her sentencing, seven

(From left to right): Thérèse Casgrain, Honorary Chair of the FFQ, René Lévesque, Louise L'Heureux, and Marie-Claire Boucher.

militants from FLF jump into the jury box, chanting anti-discrimination slogans. They create a scandal, are imprisoned...and yet, in June, the law is changed. Women can now serve as jurors.

Between the two poles embodied by FFQ and FLF, a plethora of new militant groups emerge. The year 1973 is particularly noteworthy in that respect.

In 1973, in Quebec City, Robert Bourassa's government creates the Conseil du statut de la femme (Council on the status of women). In Ottawa, Pierre Elliott Trudeau's government puts in place the Advisory Council on the Status of Women. At the same time, status of women committees are formed within large labor unions such as CSN, FTQ, and CEQ. New types of coalitions emerge: Réseau d'action et d'information pour les femmes (Women's action and information network), the collective Vidéo Femmes, Le Théâtre des Cuisines.... This is also when the series *En tant que femmes* (As women), produced by the National Film Board (NFB), is launched. Over two years and six films, directors such as Anne Claire Poirier and Mireille Dansereau will give voice to women's concerns: relationships, education, abortion.... It's a first.

In addition, in the 1970s, university courses dedicated to women are created. At Université du Québec à Montréal (UQAM), the first course is offered in 1972. Université de Montréal follows in 1978, while Concordia University aims even higher by creating the Simone de Beauvoir Institute that same year.

This intellectual exuberance leads in 1982 to a major work, the first of its kind, intended for the general public: *L'Histoire des femmes au Québec depuis quatre siècles*[2] (The history of Quebec women over the last four centuries). It is authored by four female historians—Micheline Dumont, Marie Lavigne, Michèle Stanton, and Jennifer Stoddart—who call themselves Collectif Clio.

In the same period women set important legal challenges in motion. For instance, in the early 1970s, Indigenous women asked courts to strike down provisions of the Indian Act, which revoked their status under that Act when they married non-status men. This did not happen to Indigenous

2. Collectif Clio, *L'Histoire des femmes au Québec depuis quatre siècles*, (Montréal: Quinze, Collection Idéelles, 1992), and *Feminism à la Québécoise* by Micheline Dumont, trans. by Nicole Kennedy, 2012.

men when they married non-status women. Other cases deal with sexual harassment and systemic discrimination in the workplace.

Also, more and more women in Quebec enter the workforce. Slowly, laws catch up with this new reality, sanctioning maternity leave and the need to protect pregnant women against discrimination.

The increased presence of women in the public sphere is reflected in the number of elected officials. While Claire Kirkland-Casgrain and Lise Bacon, first elected in 1973, both sat alone at the National Assembly, in 1976, five female representatives are elected at once. In the elections of September 1989, there are twenty-three. A solidarity that transcends parties brings them together when they deal with issues affecting women.

Lise Bacon's press conference at the Queen Elizabeth Hotel on February 23, 1974.

A prime example comes in the spring of 1989, when the minister responsible for women's issues, Liberal Monique Gagnon-Tremblay, introduces a new bill on family patrimony. Too many women have lost everything in a divorce. Regardless of their matrimonial regime, they should be entitled to their fair share of the property acquired during marriage when they separate.

The project is controversial even within the government. In an exceptional gesture, all the female representatives, both on the Liberal and Parti Québécois side—a total of eighteen women—band together. Thanks to their efforts, the law is passed at the very end of the parliamentary session, on June 21, 1989.

At the heart of militant feminism: the right to abortion

The core concern of militant feminism at that time is abortion—because of a fierce legal battle that took place in the late 1960s. The battle will last over twenty years, until the summer of 1989.

In 1967, Pierre Elliott Trudeau, then Minister of Justice in Pearson's government, announces the legalization of divorce, and the decriminalization of homosexuality and therapeutic abortion. It's only a half-victory, however, because abortions must be performed in authorized hospitals and are only granted under strict conditions. Few women have access to them.

In Quebec, as in Ontario, groups of women, as well as Dr. Morgentaler, decide to bypass the restrictions by opening their own clinics. Morgentaler publicly admits that he's performing illegal abortions. In 1970, he's arrested in Montreal. It's the beginning of a long legal saga that will take him to prison. Meanwhile, feminist demonstrations for the right to abortion increase. Starting in 1971, every International Women's Day (March 8), the Comité de lutte pour l'avortement et la contraception libres et gratuits (The committee to fight for free and fair abortion and contraception) holds rallies about this issue.

'The Morgentaler Affair,' as it's commonly known, lasts a long time and there are so many unusual twists and turns that it's now part of Canadian legal history. When the saga eventually comes to an end, on

January 28, 1988, the Supreme Court rules that the *Criminal Code* provisions restricting abortion are unconstitutional.

Even better, in the summer of 1989, the Supreme Court overturns rulings by the Superior Court of Justice, then the Quebec Court of Appeal, which granted a father, Jean-Guy Tremblay, the right to prevent his girlfriend, Chantal Daigle, from getting an abortion. A groundswell of support builds up around the 21-year-old woman, culminating in a protest with 10,000 demonstrators in Montreal on July 26, 1989.

The case is a hot-button issue that's not without surprises, including a spectacular *coup de théâtre*. While the legal battle is underway, Daigle goes to Boston incognito to get an abortion. The Supreme Court judges, called back from vacation to study the case, find this out on August 8, while they're holding a hearing.

Once they have recovered from the shock, they decide to continue their work. "After the Morgentaler [Affair], [a year earlier], it was almost necessary. We had to determine whether a fetus has rights," says former judge Claire L'Heureux-Dubé, who was then sitting on the Supreme Court, thirty years later.[3]

The verdict is reached on the same day, August 8, and it's unanimous: the injunction requested by Tremblay to prevent Daigle from getting an abortion is dismissed. But it takes a few more weeks to find out the grounds for the judges' decision. The report is made public in November 1989 and the conclusion is unequivocal—women have sole control over their body.

In 1989, twenty years of battles culminate with a huge victory for the feminist movement.

3. Magdaline Boutros, "Dans les coulisses de la cause Tremblay c. Daigle" [A backstage look at the case Tremblay v. Daigle], *Le Devoir*, July 17, 2019 (my translation).

Over 10,000 people marched in the streets of Montreal to pressure governments to grant women the right to abortion.

Dr. Henry Morgentaler during pro-abortion demonstrations.

Chantal Daigle in a press conference.

A LONG LIST OF PIONEERS

In addition to the militant movement of 1969–1989, "first women" in all sectors of Quebec society systematically break the glass ceiling. Naming a few of them is already drawing an impressive pantheon.

1969 First woman judge of the Superior Court of Quebec (and first woman to be appointed to a superior court in Canada): **Réjane Laberge-Colas**

1970 First woman recipient of a Prix du Québec: author **Gabrielle Roy**

1970 First woman president of the Montreal Catholic School Commission: **Thérèse Lavoie-Roux**

1972 First woman director of a non-documentary feature film: **Mireille Dansereau**, with *La vie rêvée*

1974 Thirty-two women are sworn in with the Royal Canadian Mounted Police as their first female officers

1975 First woman police officer at Sûreté du Québec: **Nicole Juteau**

1977 First woman municipal bus driver: **Francine Maltais**, in Montréal

1978 First woman commercial airline pilot: **Judy Evans-Cameron** (Air Canada)

1979 First woman judge of the Court of Appeal of Quebec: **Claire L'Heureux-Dubé**

1979 First woman police officer in the Montreal Urban Community Police: **Christiane Forcier**

1980 First woman speaker of the House of Commons: **Jeanne Sauvé**

1982 First woman General Delegate of Quebec abroad: **Michèle Thibodeau-DeGuire** in Boston

1984 First woman host of a sports radio show: **Danielle Rainville**, at CKAC

1985 First woman leader of a municipal political party: **Andrée Boucher** (Action Sainte-Foy)

1985 First woman CEO of the Montreal Urban Community Transit Corporation: **Louise Roy**

1986 First woman firefighter: **Monique Lanteigne**

1986 First woman president of a Chamber of Commerce: **Manon R. Vennat**, at the Montreal Board of Trade

1987 First woman warden of a penitentiary: **Lily Tronche**, at the Federal Training Center, formerly Saint-Vincent-de-Paul Penitentiary

1988 First woman president of a Labor Union: **Lorraine Pagé**, at the Centrale de l'enseignement du Québec

1988 First woman CEO of a television network...in North America: **Françoise Bertrand**, at Radio-Québec

Everywhere, women come together, take action, and yet very few of them publicly claim to be feminist. But is the label necessary? Feminism is associated with militant activism and, on a day-to-day basis, most Québécoises don't have the time or the brain space for it. Still, it doesn't prevent change from happening!

Let's imagine three sisters coming of age during the 1970s and 1980s: Martine, Nicole, and Annie.

Or, let's first imagine their mother—we'll call her Huguette—and come back to 1969.

Huguette is a homemaker who loves her husband, Roger. It would never occur to her to fight for anything. Yet, every Tuesday night, she sits in front of the television and follows the crazy adventures of Dodo and Denise, two self-sufficient, single women from the show *Moi et l'autre*, which airs on Radio-Canada. The show enjoys a huge success from 1966 to 1971. Like all of Quebec, Huguette is tickled by these young women who are nothing like her.

Another artist really makes her laugh: Clémence Desrochers. In 1969, this crazy comedian presents a show whose very title packs a punch: *Les Girls*. For months, Desrochers tours the show across the province, accompanied by other well-known artists—Louise Latraverse, Diane Dufresne, Chantal Renaud, and Paule Bayard (the voice of the famous puppet Bobinette in *Bobino*, the leading youth television show at the time). Critics are mixed, but the public love its stars so people show up. Huguette is among them and she applauds Desrochers and her group for their portrayal of today's women.

In the sports section of the media, between the accomplishments of the Canadiens and the Expos, with a large parenthesis for the 1976 Summer Olympics in Montreal, new figures appear. Among them, women. In 1973, even Roger pays attention to the accomplishments of Jocelyne Bourassa, the champion golfer. There's also great interest in Jacqueline Gareau, winner of the 1980 Boston Marathon. She's the first Quebec athlete to achieve this feat since…1940, when Gérard Côté finished first. On top of that, Gareau breaks the record for the fastest time ever run by a woman! Even

Dominique Michel
and Denise
Filiatrault in *Moi
et l'autre.*

Huguette, not sports inclined in the least, is happy to see her make the headlines.

Huguette doesn't need to know the long list of activities planned in Quebec to be aware that the United Nations (UN) designated 1975 as International Women's Year. She only has to turn on the radio and listen to the popular singer France Castel perform: "C'est l'Année de la femme, je sens que j'ai des ailes / Ne m'appelez plus madame, appelez-moi mademoiselle. (It's International Women's Year, I feel like I have wings / Don't call me Mrs. anymore, call me Miss.)"

Nicole, her middle daughter, doesn't agree: No more Misses! Get with the program, Mom! Now it's Ms.

Nicole is not militant but she's a big supporter of the feminist cause. In 1975, she's twenty. A subscriber to *Le Devoir*, she loves the new column created for this special year. Written by Renée Rowan, its title, "Féminin pluriel" (Feminine plural), sets the tone: it will be about women's issues.

Surprise! Once International Women's Year is over, the column disappears. Like many others, Nicole complains to the newspaper. A week later, the column is back...and will stay for the next decade.

Of course, Nicole is one of the first to read *L'Euguélionne*, a robustly original feminist novel by Quebec author Louky Bersianik, published in 1976.[4] The aim of the book is nothing less than to question everything, to "move the world a few millimeters towards the feminine" (my translation). What a breath of fresh air!

As soon as it comes out in 1978, Nicole buys *L'Agenda des femmes*, published by Éditions du remue-ménage, founded in 1976. This will become a yearly ritual as *L'Agenda* is still published to this day.

Nicole also never misses an issue of the feminist magazine *La Vie en rose* (LVR), which becomes independent in 1981 after having been an insert in the quarterly *Le Temps fou* for a year. What's great about LVR is that it's more radical than the popular women's magazine *Châtelaine*. But Nicole knows that *Châtelaine* is politically engaged too. Her mother, who buys it, often shares her impressions with her.

And Nicole goes out a lot, sometimes dragging her boyfriend of the moment along. That's how one of them sees *La Nef des sorcières* (published

Actresses in *Les Girls*: Chantal Renaud and Clémence Desrochers (front), Louise Latraverse, Paule Bayard, and Diane Dufresne (back).

4. Louky Bersianik, *L'Euguélionne* (Montréal: *La Presse*, 1976; Montréal: Typo, 2012).

in English as *A clash of symbols*) at Théâtre du Nouveau Monde (TNM) in 1976. The play features Louisette Dussault, Michèle Magny, and Luce Guilbault with texts by Marie-Claire Blais, Pol Pelletier, Nicole Brossard, and four other female writers.

Two years later, accompanied by a different boyfriend, she attends a performance of *Les fées ont soif* (published in English as *The Fairies are Thirsty*) by Denise Boucher at TNM with, again, Michèle Magny and Louisette Dussault, joined by Sophie Clément.

She leaves the play excited while the boyfriend mostly enjoys getting a taste of the controversy. Not only did the Conseil des arts de Montréal (Montreal arts council) threaten to withdraw its funding to TNM to protest the play (which exposes three female stereotypes: the Mother, the Virgin, and the Whore), but Christian fundamentalists tried to close it down, demonstrating and appealing to the courts. The company and the artistic director of TNM, Jean-Louis Roux, stand their ground—and win. The simple act of going to see the play becomes an act of resistance.

Martine, Nicole's big sister, openly admits that this attempt at censorship is nonsense. But she still finds her little sister kind of intense.

Martine got married in 1973. She was twenty-three, the average age for a Québécoise to get married back then. And get married, they certainly did! Half of the women born around 1950, like Martine, are married at twenty-five. That's impressive but it's fewer than five years earlier, when seventy percent of women born in 1945–1946 were married at twenty-five, as well as more than half of the men.

As soon as she's married, Martine gets pregnant. She wants children, so despite abortion being a hot debate, for her, it's not an option. But still, she deplores the fact that women who need it, like her cousin Louise, have to take a bus to Plattsburgh, New York, on the other side of the border, to get it.

Martine, a young teacher, has invested too much in her studies to consider staying home once she has children. Gone are the 1960s, when school boards required female teachers getting married to leave their job and focus on their family.

She's very happy to be one of the first workers to enjoy a paid maternity leave. Starting in 1971, women are allowed fifteen weeks of time off thanks

Actors Michèle Magny and Louisette Dussault during a performance of *Les fées ont soif* at TNM in November 1978.

Protests against *Les fées ont soif* on December 14, 1978.

to unemployment insurance benefits paid by Ottawa. Getting your job back when you return, however, is not always guaranteed but luckily for Martine, the issue doesn't come up.

In 1978, she has a second child...barely missing enhancements to the federal program made by the Quebec government starting January 1, 1979. Maternity leave is extended to eighteen weeks and dismissal because of a pregnancy is now banned.

In 1981, there's further progress, which Martine supports: pregnant women must be assigned a different task if their work presents a risk for the pregnancy. If reassignment is impossible, they get to stay home. The policy, put in place by René Lévesque's Parti Québécois government, is known by the name "preventive withdrawal."

That same year, a major reform of family law in the new *Civil Code* of Quebec leaves her skeptical. This reform establishes equality between spouses, which makes sense. But now, married women have to keep their maiden names, and that irritates her as much as it upsets her mother, Huguette. They were proud of having taken their husband's name—why force them to give it up?

In addition, women are now able to give their last name to their children, either alone, or in combination with the father's name. Hello hyphenated names! Martine can already imagine what her student lists will look like....

"Get with it, sis!" says Nicole, rolling her eyes. No, the word "feminist" will not come out of Martine's mouth.

In 1975, Nicole tries to shake her eldest sister out of her very conventional mindset by taking her to see the play *Môman travaille pas, a trop d'ouvrage* (Mommy doesn't work, she's too busy), presented by Théâtre des cuisines. The subtext is clear: All right, you work. But you're far from being liberated!

She tries again the following year in a more roundabout way. She takes Martine to the opening of the brand new Complexe Desjardins—an office tower that doubles as a mall—in downtown Montreal. For the occasion, sculptor Francine Larivée is presenting her large installation, *La Chambre nuptiale*, on the plaza. Over a hundred life-size figures, spread over three rooms, depict feminine and masculine stereotypes, as well as the communication problems that arise between them…"This Nicole, always so subtle!" sighs Martine, who has no desire to fight with her husband about household chores.

Martine is more concerned with the issue of violence against women, which is starting to emerge. In the 1970s, the first shelters for women victim of domestic violence open their doors, as do the first rape crisis centers.

Like her mother, Martine remembers a former neighbor, shy and withdrawn, who, a few months after her husband's death, as she was getting ready to move, spoke out about his mistreatment of her. What? This friendly neighbor beat his wife? They were shocked and embarrassed to not have seen it, to not have understood.

In 1979, *Mourir à tue-tête* (*A Scream from Silence*), a film about rape by Anne Claire Poirier, hits Martine like a punch in the face. It presents a realistic depiction of the assault and its repercussions on a young nurse. Reality, seen by a woman, and suddenly projected on a big screen, is frightening….

The year 1979 is an important year for feminist films. Nicole sees everything: all the works of Anne Claire Poirier, of course, but also *L'Arrache-coeur* (Heartsnatcher) by Mireille Dansereau, *La Cuisine rouge* by Paule Baillargeon and Frédérique Collin, *Cordélia* by Jean Beaudin, featuring Louise Portal, and the documentaries *Les Servantes du bon Dieu* (in English: *The Handmaidens of God*) by Diane Létourneau, and *Une naissance apprivoisée* by Michel Moreau…. Not to mention the birth of Théâtre expérimental des femmes, with Pol Pelletier.

Martine, for her part, is more interested in television. Two series featuring strong female characters, owners of a small business, launch in 1979: *Chez Denise* by Denise Filiatrault, and *Caroline* by Marcelle Racine, with the great Catherine Bégin in the leading role. Martine is hooked, just like three years later, in 1982, she will be hooked to the series *La Bonne Aventure* by Lise Payette. This last series is overtly feminist, reflecting its author, a former star radio host and former minister in Lévesque's government, notably for the Status of Women.

The year 1982 is also when the pin-up on page seven of *Journal de Montréal* finally disappears. Undressing young women for the readers'

pleasure is no longer appropriate. Nicole is delighted, and this time, both Huguette and Martine agree.

Louise Portal in the film *Cordélia,* directed by Jean Beaudin.

Annie watches her older sisters but remains unfazed. She's the youngest. Born in 1965, she belongs to another generation of women. Of course, she'll carve her own path. Now everything is possible!

Besides, the pioneers who have opened the doors of fields until then closed to women—like sports coverage, the police, the construction industry—did so to fulfill a passion, not to carry the torch of equality. That's what they say when they're interviewed by journalists.

So, in this year 1987, when Annie goes for a beer with her girlfriends, neither feminism nor gender equality enter their discussion. They don't even see the irony in their favorite meeting spot being a former tavern which, five years earlier, was forbidden to women—though the law banning men-only institutions had been passed in 1979.

Annie doesn't waste any time on this because the past is over. Now, as Cyndi Lauper has triumphally been singing since 1983, "Girls Just Want to

Have Fun." The future promises to be bright—she is about to finish her undergraduate degree in Electrical Engineering at Montreal's École Polytechnique and already has a job lined up.

Engineering...a good choice to escape the protective gaze of her two big sisters. They know nothing about it! But recently, they've been leaving her alone. Martine still works but she's questioning her relationship. Her midlife crisis must be approaching.

As for Nicole, on top of her busy legal practice, she's become involved with the Bar of Quebec. The legal world is opening up to women, but there's a great need to raise awareness, especially among male colleagues. She also talks more and more about having a baby "on her own." It seems easier to her than to keep looking for the "perfect" father.

Annie doesn't feel concerned with these personal and professional upheavals. She's confident about her career choice and she knows her boyfriend understands the concept of gender equality. A few months earlier, didn't he, like her, give a standing ovation to La La La Human Steps for their show *Human Sex*? In a stunning, high-energy choreography, the star dancer, Louise Lecavalier, literally carried her partner, Marc Béland.

Annie appreciated the metaphor. Things are changing but it's just a matter of adjusting—we'll all move on without even having to talk about it.

La La La
Human Steps

BREWING DISCOMFORT

There are lofty ideals and then there's reality. The solid ground. The grass-roots level. A traditional foundation that's not necessarily an old foundation, but rather the bedrock on which most of Quebec society still rests.

It's true for men, but also for women. The discomfort that some of them feel in the face of all the changes will blow up spectacularly in 1980. It will have a name: Yvette.

That spring, René Lévesque's Parti Québécois government puts its plan into action. In May 1980, voters will have to answer a long and complicated question, which in the end is simple.

For or against Quebec sovereignty? In the Yes camp or in the No camp?

The two sides present their arguments. In early March, on International Women's Day, Lise Payette, Minister of State for the Status of Women and a self-proclaimed feminist, introduces a new argument. She compares the emancipation of Quebec to that of women, long relegated to housework, as shown in an excerpt from an old schoolbook where a young boy named Guy is engaged in the world while his sister Yvette, "happy and sweet," helps around the house. The next day, the Minister goes further by pointing out that the leader of the No camp, Liberal Claude Ryan, "is married to an Yvette." Her comment is condemned in a powerful article by Lise Bissonnette, then editor-in-chief of *Le Devoir*.

This is a turning point for the referendum campaign. Yet, pushback doesn't initially come from the all-male leaders of the No camp; it comes from "ordinary" women Liberal activists, homemakers who feel scorned by the big feminist shakeup. In late March, in less than 24 hours and minimally supported by party officials, they organize a "brunch of Yvettes" in Quebec City.

The success is such that, despite the skepticism of their male colleagues, veteran female Liberal organizers decide to do the same thing in Montreal.

As it turns out, the interest is so great that the organizers pick the Montreal Forum as the gathering place. On the evening of April 7, 1980, 15,000 women show up. On stage are a number of important women

(On the left): Claude Ryan, surrounded by a group of women during the evening of Yvettes at the Montreal Forum, on April 7, 1980.

politicians including Thérèse Casgrain, the emblematic figure of first-wave feminism.

The Montreal gathering is followed by more than fifty meetings of Yvettes in different regions of Quebec, which take place right up until the referendum of May 20. The defense of federalism gives an opportunity to women to explore other tensions until then hidden from public view....

In the workplace, also shaken by the new feminist order, those tensions are not even hidden, and women are saddled with the burden of enduring them. Yet, few dare to talk about the situation publicly. They reason that it will go away, or that it's best to conserve their energy for the long run.

Nonetheless, as soon as she leaves politics, the formidable Lise Payette shares her disappointing experience in her book *Le pouvoir? Connais pas!* (Power? Don't know what it is), published in 1982.[5] She recounts the sexist attitude of her colleagues, and the difficulty for a woman, even as strong-willed and well-known as she is, to carve her place in politics—ultimately a man's world.

In October 1981, another exposé appears under the title "Le cinéma féminin au Québec" (Women's cinema in Quebec) in the magazine *Copie zéro* published by Cinémathèque québécoise. Professor Jocelyne Denault describes the conditions at the NFB in the early 1970s, when women producers were working on the series *En tant que femmes*, which was to be the feminist poster child for the organization. As Denault explains: "It was a candy thrown to women by the National Film Board (NFB) in preparation for International Women's Year."

Because in reality, what paternalism there is at NFB! It ranges from stupid jokes ("Try to at least hire beautiful women") to distrust of the topics chosen by the group (male colleagues don't find them important enough or see them as too narrowly focused...).

"These reactions are followed by aggression on the men's part: there's fear that women will take these gentlemen's places." So, disparaging remarks abound ("All right, go ahead girls, we'll give you a hand"), as well as demands for greater performance. All of that in a field that defines itself as progressive.

5. Lise Payette, *Le pouvoir? Connais pas!* (Montreal: Québec Amérique, 1982).

What Denault describes is universal. In a number of sectors, sexist jokes meant to ridicule or attack women are more or less part of the job... and even of training for the job. The newspaper *Le Polyscope*, published by Polytechnique students, offers a concentrated version of this behavior in each issue. It's so ingrained in the culture that most people don't even notice. Plus, anyone who complained would be seen as a bad sport—who wants that reputation?

Worse, however, is the fate of women who enter for the first time sectors previously inaccessible to them—like, for example, the police[6] and the army.[7] Despite the official discourse, their presence is not accepted. In fact, some of their male colleagues have no qualms saying so publicly when a microphone is pointed in their direction.

A news story produced by Radio-Canada in April 1980, when only three out of 3,700 drivers working for Commission de transport de la Communauté urbaine de Montréal (later the Société de transport de Montréal) were women, drives this point home.[8] The male drivers interviewed are harsh: "I'll tell you, I've never accepted that a woman gets behind the wheel." Another one: "Men have a hard-enough time getting work without women stealing their jobs from under them." And another one: "My opinion is that women are meant to stay at home. A man who respects his wife in the least keeps her at home."

6. The Royal Canadian Mounted Police (RCMP) welcomes women for the first time in 1974. In 1975, the first female police officer is hired by Sûreté du Québec, and the Institut national de police in Nicolet welcomes its first women trainees. The Montreal Urban Community Police Service hires its first female officer in 1979.

7. In 1979, Canadian Military Colleges are legally obliged to accept women. The Royal Military College of Canada in Kingston welcome its first female students in the fall of 1980. In 1986, a decision by the Canadian Human Rights Tribunal forces the army to open all of its jobs to women within ten years, except in submarines. This exception is lifted in 2001.

8. News story by Denise Gascon in the show *Ce soir* of April 3, 1980, Radio-Canada Archives, [online].

Women suffer in silence from a range of behaviors that go from debasement to pure torture. It will take years, even decades, for them to reveal everything[9] and be taken seriously.[10]

Indeed, in those years, we're barely staring to lift the veil on the dark side of the workplace for women, which includes sexual harassment. In 1980, Au bas de l'échelle, the advocacy group for non-unionized workers, forms a committee to address this issue. In 1984, the group becomes the independent organization Groupe d'aide et d'information sur le harcèlement sexuel au travail (Help and information center on sexual harassment in the workplace). But the problem makes most people smile—until it is formally recognized as an issue in a Supreme Court decision in 1989.

Even making female workers visible is its own challenge—and it's reflected in the vocabulary, because names in French are marked by gender, and at that time a lot of professions were identified only by their masculine form. Starting in 1979, in the wake of Lise Payette, who, as soon as she was elected in 1976 demanded to be called "*la ministre*" (the feminine version of "le" minister), the Office québécois de la langue française recommends the feminization of job titles. A notice is published in the *Gazette officielle du Québec*. Yet, for more than a decade, the media refuses to comply. Many commentators make fun of feminization by inventing job titles that have nothing to do with the recommendations of the Office.

In addition, the challenges of home life are still underestimated. There are more and more conversations about the division of domestic labor in couples, but things are changing at a glacial pace. Also the concept of "emotional labor" falling almost exclusively on women doesn't exist yet.

Lise Payette, host of the television show *Appelez-moi Lise (Call me Lise)*.

9. For two examples of detailed testimonials, see Sandra Perron, *Seule au front* (Montreal: Québec Amérique, 2018); Kate Armstrong, "I was the first female cadet at Royal Military College. Decades later I realized I was never 'one of the guys,' *The Star*, May 26, 2019; Nicole Juteau, first female police officer at Sûreté du Québec, also talked about her difficult beginnings in interviews given through the 2010s, saying, in particular, to *La Presse+*: "At my retirement party, many of my male colleagues offered their apologies for making my life so difficult" (my translation)—Louise Leduc, "La pionnière devenue guide" (The pioneer turned guide), *La Presse+*, September 21, 2013.

10. In 2016, and again in 2019, the RCMP announces payments totaling $200 million in compensation to female employees victims of harassment, intimidation, or assault in the workplace, with the statute of limitation going back to 1974. In July 2019, $900 million in compensation will go to victims of sexual misconduct in the Canadian Armed Forces.

As for domestic or family violence, it's still taboo. Only in 1985 does the Quebec government put in place a policy to support victims of domestic violence, but again, some people question the scale of the problem.

What's clear, however, is that women don't feel compelled to stay in failing relationships anymore, even when they have children. Between 1975 and 1985, the number of single parents doubles in Quebec. Two-thirds of separations are now initiated by women who are dissatisfied with their marriage.

What do men say? Most of them adjust as best they can. But the reaction of one Jean-Guy Tremblay, who, in the summer of 1989, wants to force his pregnant girlfriend, Chantal Daigle, to keep a child she doesn't want, to the point of taking legal procedures against her, reveals deep-seated anger, more widespread than we might have thought.

The tragedy, 1989–1991

NAMING WHAT HAPPENED

THE NIGHT OF THE POLYTECHNIQUE massacre, there was the shock, of course. Massive. Unimaginable. A shooting never before seen in Canada,[1] rare in the educational world,[2] exceptional even on the world stage.[3] And above all, it was the first time that women were targeted—what we understand today as a femicide.

And yet, this distinction is hardly mentioned in the first few hours following the massacre. The attack took place between 5:10 p.m. and 5:28 p.m. but it takes until 9:00 p.m. to find out in the news that all the deceased are women. Why this delay?

Maybe because of disbelief.

La Presse journalist Marie-Claude Lortie, on location that night, will reflect on this years later: "I remember refusing to believe the information

---

1. At that time, only five similar shootings had taken place in Canada since 1959, the worst being Denis Lortie's attack on the National Assembly in May 1984, which killed three people and injured thirteen, and to which Marc Lépine referred in the letter found on him after his death. Since then, there has been one, more damaging shooting: the murder of 22 people by a denturist in Nova Scotia, after he assaulted his common-law partner. The shootings occurred on April 18th and 19th, 2020, in seven different towns in the province, involving 16 separate crime scenes.

2. Four of the five shootings that had happened at public establishments in Canada took place in high schools (one in Alberta in 1959, two in Ontario in 1975, and one in Manitoba in 1978; the fifth shooting was the one at the National Assembly in 1984), but in every case the number of victims was limited to one or two dead and a few injured.

In the US, however, the University of Texas tower shooting had already taken place in Austin in 1966, when a gunman killed fifteen people and injured thirty-one. But it was the Columbine High School Massacre, with thirteen dead and twenty-four injured, that became the symbol of school shootings. (They have since increased in the US.) However, the Columbine shooting happened in 1999, ten years after the Polytechnique massacre.

3. On December 7, 1989, *La Presse* lists about fifteen shootings in the Western World, other than armed conflicts, that have made more than ten victims since 1949; ten of these took place in the US.

The late Pierre Leclair shows a photo of his daughter Maryse, one of the victims of the Polytechnique massacre.

Because They Were Women

indicating that all the victims were women, as intended by the shooter."[4] Similarly, a year after the tragedy, police officer Pierre Leclair, who found his daughter Maryse assassinated, said that when he entered Polytechnique, the first thing that hit him was the magnitude of the carnage. He was so shocked that, "in the moment, [he didn't] pay attention to the fact that all the victims were women."[5]

Maybe also because public space was still essentially a male space and we were struggling to adjust our vocabulary.

The reaction of then Minister of Education Claude Ryan illustrates this bias when, that night, he offers "his deepest condolences to the families of the 'étudiants' [the masculine form of the word 'student'] who have been cut down in the prime of life".[6] The next day, at the National Assembly, Premier Robert Bourassa, Leader of the Opposition Jacques Parizeau, and Leader of Equality Party Robert Libman, condemn the tragedy and offer their condolences. They talk about "victims," "youth," "loved ones," but the words "women" or "girls" are never uttered. In this way, the terrifying specificity of the tragedy remains hidden.

Alternately, maybe it was because this specificity was too difficult to accept and, right from the beginning, we had to avoid any political analysis. Twenty-five years later, journalist Shelley Page, also sent to Polytechnique that night, will remember the degree to which her bosses (all men, as was the case in the media then) didn't trust her coverage and how, whether consciously or not, she factored in their concerns.[7]

Since the tragedy took place at the end of the day, a majority of young journalists, who were the last hired and so assigned the evening shift, were sent to Polytechnique. A lot of these recent hires were women in their twenties, barely older than the students targeted by the gunman. Page wrote: "There was immediate anxiety on the news desk about having sent two young women to cover the slaughter of other women. Some editors worried

4. Marie-Claude Lortie, "Souvenirs d'un cauchemar" [*Memories of a nightmare*], *La Presse*, February 6, 2009 (my translation).

5. André Pépin, "Le monde n'est pas si méchant" [*People are not that mean*], *La Presse*, December 1, 1990 (my translation).

6. Gilles Normand, "L'Assemblée nationale se rappelle l'affaire Lortie…" [The National Assembly remembers the Lortie affair…], *La Presse*, December 7, 1989 (my translation).

7. Shelley Page, "How I sanitized the feminist outrage over the Montreal massacre," *Ottawa Citizen*, December 6, 2014.

junior reporters like us weren't up to the task; one told me he worried we wouldn't cover the story objectively."[8]

She wasn't the only female journalist to have to deal with this mistrust. It was also manifest on the air: that night, in the media both in the province and outside of Quebec, all the explaining, talking, commenting is done by men.... Feminists are so struck by this that they will constantly bring it up afterwards.

$$- \dotdiv -$$

In the end, even if four out of the fourteen people injured are men, the gunman was only targeting female students—so all of the dead are dead women.... Thus, it becomes impossible to turn a blind eye; the attack was against women.

The next day, this realization is on the front page of every newspaper: "14 morts, toutes des femmes" (14 dead, all women) claims *Le Journal de Québec* in bold red characters. Several officials also recognize this fact, denouncing violence against women, mourning the young women who chose a field traditionally reserved for men and were so brutally attacked, and pleading for equality....

In a press conference on December 7, the Mayor of Montreal, Jean Doré, is unambiguous. He underscores the misogyny of the killer and doesn't hide his sadness or his tears while talking to journalists.

Crying in public was rare for a man and unheard of for an elected official. But Mayor Doré is personally affected by the tragedy. His colleague, City Councilor Thérèse Daviau, lost her daughter Geneviève, whom he knew very well.... A year later, the Mayor will recall the press conference and reaffirm his feminist convictions: "Not everyone has followed the evolution of the last twenty years [...]. During the electoral campaign, I saw men who were offended by gender equality programs."[9]

Mayor of Montreal Jean Doré, moved to tears during the press conference held on December 7, 1989.

8. Ibid.

9. Francine Pelletier, "Qui a peur de Marc Lépine?" [Who's afraid of Marc Lépine?], *La Presse*, December 1, 1990 (my translation).

Still, on television and similarly on radio, which boast a massive following when an event like this happens,[10] the analysis is a lot more timid, both the day after the tragedy and in the following days.

On the evening of December 7, Radio-Canada television presents a special program hosted by news anchor Bernard Derome, who cut short his vacation for the occasion. Louise Cousineau, renowned television columnist at *La Presse*, is surprised: "Three men with him. They talked about violence; they barely mentioned that this terrifying violence was directed against women."[11]

The next day, she adds: "Little has been said in the coverage of the massacre about the antifeminist wave washing over North America, that the killer suddenly embodied."[12]

Case in point, it takes a few more days for Quebec to understand that the attack wasn't against women, but against feminists. Outside of Quebec, this angle is discussed as early as the day after the massacre during a debate on CBC where women are present. And it's discussed again on December 8 in the *Globe and Mail* and in American newspapers, including *USA Today*.

Given the gender of the victims and the location of the tragedy, this analysis was inevitable. Especially since Marc Lépine himself declared his hatred of feminists in the first classroom he went into, where he killed six of the nine women present. This hatred is also expressed at length in the letter he was carrying on him during the massacre.

Yet, the contents of the letter, whose existence is revealed by the police in a press conference on December 7, 1989, the day Lépine's identity is also revealed, will stay concealed for almost a year.

The day after the tragedy, we only learn that the letter comprises three handwritten pages, that Lépine announces his suicide, and that it includes a list of nineteen women he wanted to kill—well-known feminists, but also

10. Television columnist Louise Cousineau's first piece dedicated to the Polytechnique tragedy opens this way: "What to do in such moments? You learn about the tragedy on the radio, and you run to your television. Above knowing is seeing. [...] That's how it's been since the assassination of John F. Kennedy. When the order of things collapses, viewers keep watch. They're there without being there." —"Une télé qui avait du mal à bousculer ses habitudes" (How TV was struggling to change its habits), *La Presse*, December 8, 1989 (my translation).
11. Ibid.
12. Louise Cousineau, "R.-C. supprime deux films où les femmes sont massacrées" (R.-C. pulls two films where women are slaughtered), *La Presse*, December 9, 1989 (my translation).

first women to hold positions in male strongholds:[13] Lise Payette, Janette Bertrand, Monique Gagnon-Tremblay, Lorraine Pagé, Danielle Rainville, Vice-President of CSN Monique Simard... They're not identified in the press conference, but their names still end up in the media.

La Presse columnist Francine Pelletier, known as the co-founder of the feminist magazine LVR, who was targeted by Lépine, tries to obtain a copy of the letter. She first asks the MUC Police, then makes a request under the Quebec Access to Information Act. To no avail. Then in November 1990, she receives a photocopy of the letter through the mail, "without any information, totally anonymous, like in a detective novel."[14]

The letter is published on the front page of *La Presse*, on November 24, 1990. Lépine's grievances (against "viragos," which all feminists are; against women in the army; against maternity leaves; against preventive withdrawals...) leave no doubt as to the object of his obsessions.

Still, in December 1989, a few voices in Quebec manage to pierce through the dominant discourse of incomprehension in the face of Lépine's act.

On December 7, sexologist and writer Jocelyne Robert participates in a radio show on CJRT 1140 in Trois-Rivières. She was invited to discuss her most recent book on children's affective and sexual education to foster equality. However, given the recent events, the interview shifts to a round-table. "I was the only one pointing out that everything indicated we were dealing with the extreme and murderous expression of a hatred of women, a refusal of gender equality. [...] The other guests were looking at me like I was crazy."[15]

13. The media refers to "femme pompier" and "femmes policiers" (a feminization of the professions using the word "woman" in front of the masculine word instead of using the feminine version of the word) identified by Marc Lépine; Thérèse Daviau, whose daughter is one of the victims of the Polytechnique massacre, is introduced as "conseiller municipal" (the masculine version of City Councilor) in news stories. Even in such circumstances, the feminization of professions is not embraced in journalism.

14. Francine Pelletier, "Je me souviens" [I remember], *La Vie en rose*, Hors-série, 2005, 36 (my translation).

15. Jocelyne Robert, "Les Quatorze" [The Fourteen], *HuffPost Québec*, December 5, 2014 (my translation).

On December 8, on the radio show *Ici comme ailleurs* on Radio-Canada, politician and seasoned essayist Pierre Bourgault answers the questions of host Michel Désautels. He unpacks the tragedy this way:

> This is the first acknowledged sexist crime. There have been thousands of them in the history of the world, but men have always managed to not acknowledge them. There were reasons for doing this or for doing that…. It's also a political crime because it targets a specific group. […] Their only crime is to be women. […] It's been described as an isolated event […]. The event was by nature isolated but historically, it's not. It's a collective crime against women.

In mainstream media, female columnists analyze the event in the same way.

On December 9, Francine Pelletier writes in *La Presse*:[16] "It's an act of retaliation—deliberate, calculated, and directed against women in general and feminists in particular." For her part, Nathalie Petrowski writes in *Le Devoir*:[17] "How can we explain that the shooter only killed women […]. No one could explain it, no one could understand. Did they have their heads stuck in the sand? […] [The shooter] aimed with all the strength of his misogyny."

Marie-Claude Lortie, then a 24-year-old reporter, pens a very personal article in *La Presse,* feeling that in such circumstances, it's essential to go beyond journalistic objectivity. She concludes: "Afraid of what we would say, afraid of what we would ignore [….] Afraid that our fathers, our friends, our brothers wouldn't react, once again. That they would continue to believe that we're paranoid. That they would again refuse to hear us tell them that we're afraid of being raped, of being beaten, of being killed by those who don't understand."[18]

Journalist
Francine Pelletier.

16. Francine Pelletier, "On achève bien les chevaux, n'est-ce pas?" [They shoot horses, don't they?], *La Presse*, December 9, 1989 (my translation).
17. Nathalie Petrowski, "Chaperon rouge" [Red riding hood], *Le Devoir*, December 9, 1989 (my translation).
18. Marie-Claude Lortie, "Tristesse, tristesse" [Sadness, sadness], *La Presse*, December 11, 1989 (my translation).

On December 10, a demonstration in Montreal organized by the Coalition Québécoise pour le droit à l'avortement libre et gratuit, (Quebec Coalition for the Right to Free Abortion), which was already planned, becomes an opportunity for thirty-five women and five men to condemn the Polytechnique tragedy, violence against women, and the way in which many try to minimize the antifeminist implications of what happened.[19]

Commentators follow, in particular *Le Devoir* editorial writer Jean-Claude Leclerc, who rejects the catch-all argument of increasing violence. Instead, he says: "The young killer [...] wasn't against women in general (he didn't kill nurses or restaurant waitresses), but against those who embodied new women carving a place for themselves in a still very male world. The message was clear. Few feminists were duped. The attack was on 'women's liberation.'"[20]

But he immediately adds: "Should we understand this as the threat of a 'male power' channeled by the shooter, a performer more spectacular but barely less violent than wife beaters? It's here that the analysis becomes more complicated, and an error of interpretation could very well lead to more tragedies."

It's most of all here that the debate heats up.

19. Raymond Gervais, "Les féministes dénoncent la misogynie des hommes et de leurs gouvernements" [Feminists denounce the misogyny of men and their governments], *La Presse*, December, 1989; Renée Rowan, "Chantal Daigle s'identifie aux 14 victimes de Poly" [Chantal Daigle identifies with the 14 victims from Polytechnique], *Le Devoir*, December 11, 1989.

20. Jean-Claude Leclerc, "Les raisons d'une tragédie" [The reasons for a tragedy], *Le Devoir*, December 11, 1989 (my translation).

INTERPRETING WHAT HAPPENED

Should the massacre perpetrated by Marc Lépine be attributed to a single man, a "crazy shooter," as he is painted in the media, or to a misogynist representative of the male violence coursing through society? Unless this man was driven to crime by feminism itself?

These questions stir passions. For weeks, they feed editorials and columns, debates, call-in radio shows, and op-eds.

Opinions are split along a clear line and culminate in two publications with drastically divergent perspectives. First, *Polytechnique, 6 décembre*, an anthology comprising several women contributors, is published by Éditions du remue-ménage in the spring of 1990.[21] It is answered by the uncompromising and much noticed *Manifeste d'un salaud* (The bad guy manifesto) by journalist Roch Côté, published in the fall of 1990.[22]

A new polarization emerges: masculinists against feminists, and vice versa. In each camp, anger is deep, accusations are harsh, and arguments are elaborate.

Lépine's act lifted a taboo. In the hours following the tragedy, men share their understanding and even their approval of him. Thirty years later, Nathalie Provost, one of the survivors in classroom C-230.4, where Lépine first opened fire killing six female students and injuring three others, vividly remembers.[23]

She stood up to this young man armed with a rifle who was telling them that he hated feminists. "Come on, we're not feminists, we didn't take anyone's place," she more or less told him.[24]

But when she is hospitalized for her injuries, she hears men on the radio saying that Lépine did a good thing. Stunned, she decides to meet with journalists in order to communicate something fundamental to her that she feels is her responsibility since she's involved in the Polytechnique Students' Association (AEP) and sits on the board of the school.

---

21. Marie Chalouh and Louise Malette (ed.), *Polytechnique, 6 décembre* (Montréal: Éditions du remue-ménage, 1990).

22. Roch Côté, *Manifeste d'un salaud* (Terrebonne: Éditions du Portique, 1990).

23. Meeting with Nathalie Provost, June 19, 2019 (my translation).

24. Nathalie Collard, Katia Gagnon, "Quatre femmes, quatre bilans" [Four women, four analyses], *La Presse*, December 6, 2014 (my translation).

On Friday, December 8, she holds a short press conference from her hospital bed that is so unusual that the journalists applaud her afterwards.[25] She says: "To all the young women in Quebec who were thinking about studying engineering, I'm asking you to consider this career with as much enthusiasm as you did before Wednesday." Above all, she didn't want anyone to look for a guilty party other than Marc Lépine: "There's only one culprit and he's dead."

Experts, commentators, the vast majority of elected officials, and many members of the public—and not just men—plead for Lépine's act to not be overinvested with meaning. Incidentally, Lépine is found to have had a miserable childhood within a complicated family, ruled by a violent father.

Among them, Pierre Foglia, the most popular columnist of the time and a prominent figure in Quebec journalism, makes his point in his typical frank and direct style. Relating the comments of a neighbor who thought Lépine was friendly, Foglia writes: "If you manage to make a monster out of that, it's because you have a talent for psychology. Or feminism. Or journalism... [...] If you don't, maybe it's because there's no monster. Only ordinary men and women, like you and me. Anyone can miss a step and fall into madness."[26]

Analyzing the personality of the killer is the privileged approach—but the media doesn't call on feminists who specialize in questions of violence against women to weigh in.

This is largely condemned by militant feminists and feminist allies, who see another way to annihilate the effect that the shooting had on women. The shooting was, in fact, "an extreme expression of daily violence."[27]

The anthology *Polytechnique, 6 décembre* captures their anger and pain. A passage perfectly summarizes the spirit of the book, comprised of

25. Paul Roy, "Il y a un seul coupable et il est mort" [There's only one culprit and he's dead], *La Presse*, December 9, 1989 (my translation).

26. Pierre Foglia, "Quel monstre?" [What Monster?], *La Presse*, December 9, 1989 (my translation).

27. Mélissa Blais, "Entre la folie d'un seul homme et les violences faites aux femmes: la mémoire collective du 6 décembre 1989," Master's thesis (Université du Québec à Montréal: 2007) (my translation).

fifty contributions: "Initially considered public, the act was quickly reduced to a family fight that got out of control and moved into the private sphere. In doing so, a new form of violence was inflicted on thousands of women who had 'wrongly' felt wounded at their core."[28]

Another comment reveals the deep fear felt by many women, yet ignored in the coverage of the event. During a "brunch reflection" about the massacre organized in January 1990 by the Fédération professionnelle des journalistes du Québec (FPJQ), Anne-Marie Dussault, then host of *Le Point* on Radio-Canada television, says: "The day after the Polytechnique tragedy, I met with City of Montreal female blue collar workers for a news story [...]. The meeting had been scheduled for two weeks. That morning, at least a dozen terrorized women refused to speak on camera. They felt hunted, in danger, and they were completely overwhelmed."[29]

Historian Mélissa Blais dedicated her Master's thesis to the Polytechnique massacre, as well as a book titled *J'haïs les féministes!* (I hate feminists!) published in 2009 by Éditions du remue-ménage.[30] She also co-edited the collection *Retour sur un attentat antiféministe*, published in 2010.[31] Her conclusion is unequivocal: "The use of this kind of [psychological] expertise allows journalists to bring Lépine's act down to the level of the individual, and in doing so, to present it as if it were exceptional. Comparative analyses of different crimes committed specifically against women, and analyses looking for explanations within social relationships are put aside or drowned out by the comments of male experts (but far fewer women experts) working in the field of psychology. The significant number of articles about Lépine's familial and psycho-emotional difficulties encourage readers to adopt a discourse that psychologizes the events of December 6, 1989."[32]

28. Sylvie Bérard, "Mots et gestes," *Polytechnique, 6 décembre*, op. cit., 75 (my translation).

29. Virginie Boulanger, "Avons-nous bien couvert la tragédie de Poly ?" [Did we cover the Polytechnique tragedy well?], *Le 30*, March 1990 (my translation).

30. Mélissa Blais, *J'haïs les féministes!* (Montréal: Éditions du remue-ménage, 2009).

31. Mélissa Blais, Francis Dupuis-Déri, Lyne Kurtzman and Dominique Payette (ed.), *Retour sur un attentat antiféministe. École polytechnique de Montréal, 6 décembre 1989* (Montréal: Éditions du remue-ménage, 2010).

32. Mélissa Blais, "Entre la folie d'un seul homme et les violences faites aux femmes: la mémoire collective du 6 décembre 1989," op. cit., 123 (my translation).

On the flip side, some people accuse feminists of instrumentalizing the tragedy, of mixing everything, and of generalizing too much. It's sometimes said carefully, but most of the time, it sounds like an accusation.

Le Manifeste by Roch Côté is a good example. The book denounces "Le procès de l'homme" (The trial of man), which is the title of one of the chapters. It provides fodder for discussion, even vigorous debate, but Côté expresses his point of view with hostility. He even directly attacks feminist personalities while failing to mention that these women were on Lépine's list of women to kill. From being prey, the women become predator. It's a complete reversal of perspective that Blais analyses in detail in her work.

At that time and long afterwards, many women will insist on correcting this perspective, like Lise Payette who, as recently as 2016, explained that after the Polytechnique massacre, "men managed to make everyone believe that [feminism] was violent. [...] We talk a lot about the Quiet Revolution, but the only quiet revolution I know is the women's revolution. Women didn't go into men's schools to shoot them. Feminism is not violent. It fights for women's rights but doesn't want to take them away from men."[33]

A step backward

The December 1989 tragedy slows the militant movement down to a crawl. "All feminists were not assassinated, but [all of them] were profoundly hurt by the event," says Payette in 2016, adding that it took two years for the feminist message to find its legs again.

The historical thread of Quebec's feminist movement[34] proves her right. The years 1990 and 1991 are almost dead calm, except for the long-planned celebrations of the 50th anniversary of women's right to vote in Quebec, new provisions for a parental leave without pay as part of the Act

33. Annabelle Blais, "Lise Payette, le féminisme revanchard et alors?" [Lise Payette, angry feminism...so what?], *Journal de Montréal*, February 13, 2016.
34. Réseau québécois en études féministes, *Ligne du temps de l'histoire des femmes au Québec, 1600 à nos jours*, histoiredesfemmes.quebec.

Respecting Labour Standards, and the nomination of a few "first women."[35] We are very, very far from the exuberance of the previous two decades.

Worse, a controversy that everyone thought settled resurfaces: abortion.

Following a decision from the Supreme Court in 1988, abortion is not constrained anymore, and this legal vacuum seems unacceptable to the Conservative government of Brian Mulroney. The Prime Minister sets up an internal committee to address this issue, within which—we'll find out twenty-five years later[36]—ministers will engage in an epic debate. The hard-liners win.

In November 1989, Bill C-43 is introduced in the House of Commons: it imposes severe restrictions on abortion, banning any termination of pregnancy unless a doctor rules that the life or the health of the mother is threatened. Despite protests and demonstrations, it is adopted on May 23, 1990 during a free vote of 140 to 131, although it would be defeated in the Senate the following year. Yet only a few months earlier, the Supreme Court had recognized that women had the right to control their own bodies.... It's a huge step backward.

The phrase "le compteur a été remis à zero" (the counter was reset to zero) found in one of the contributions to *Polytechnique, 6 décembre*,[37] doesn't solely concern the massacre anymore but is applicable to the entire feminist movement.

35. Lise Bissonnette takes the lead of *Le Devoir*, the first woman to head a daily newspaper in Quebec; Léa Cousineau becomes the first woman chair of the City of Montreal executive committee; Louise Fréchette is the first woman appointed Canada's Ambassador to the UN.

36. Stanley Stromp, "Avortement—Des documents de l'ère Mulroney lèvent le voile sur un débat houleux" [Abortion—Mulroney-era cabinet documents reveal struggle to replace abortion law thrown out by court], *La Presse canadienne*, November 17, 2013.

37. Marie-Thérèse Bournival, "Quand le vernis craque" [When the veneer cracks], *Polytechnique, 6 décembre*, op. cit., 70.

At first, the public debate about the meaning of the Polytechnique massacre seems endless. But less than six months later, other polarizing issues completely eclipse it.

On May 22, 1990, ten years after the lost referendum of 1980, Lucien Bouchard, federal Minister of the Environment, causes a shock by resigning from Brian Mulroney's Conservative government to sit as an independent. He's followed by six other Members of Parliament (MPs), both Conservative and Liberal, who, together that summer, form a federal sovereigntist party—Bloc Québécois. A first MP, Gilles Duceppe, is elected under this banner in a by-election in August.

This causes massive turmoil. In June 1990, the Meech Lake Accord, which was intended to persuade Quebec to endorse the *Constitution Act, 1982*, is defeated just as it was on the verge of being adopted. The summer of 1990 is politically tumultuous.

It's also tumultuous on another, completely unanticipated front: Indigenous claims. At the end of April, Mohawks from Kanesatake erect a barricade on the road leading to the Oka golf course. They're protesting the expansion of the golf course and the construction of a housing development on their claimed traditional lands. The confrontation comes to a head at the beginning of July, leading to the death of a police officer and the establishment of a siege on the Indigenous side. The Oka Crisis, as it is called, makes the headlines until the end of September 1990 and provokes heated responses.

The Polytechnique tragedy is also eclipsed because a majority of the population sees it as a reason for sadness and pain rather than an opportunity to make demands. And the "people from Polytechnique," those who witnessed the massacre, are not interested in fueling the debate, and much less in feeding the media.

At the end of January 1990, several journalists attend FPJQ's "brunch reflection." Relatives of the victims are present. "The room is bursting with emotion," the monthly magazine *Le 30*, published by the Fédération, reports in its March issue.

One of the injured students, Geneviève Cauden, and Jimmy Edward, brother of Anne-Marie Edward, who was killed by Lépine, condemn the journalists' work. "During these accusations, inconspicuous in the audience, Polytechnique students who had come incognito to support them were crying silently."[38]

The first anniversary of the massacre confirms this mistrust.

As part of an imposing series of articles that *La Presse* is dedicating to the event, reporter Michèle Ouimet is sent to Polytechnique. After walking around the school, she writes: "Marc Lépine's shadow is absent."[39] Instead, what emerges from her conversations with people is exasperation with all the media hype. "Students and professors [...] are unanimous. Enough with the media!"[40]

But the desire to talk internally doesn't seem to exist either, notes the journalist. "Even those who were there don't bring it up. It seems taboo," a new student tells her, surprised. "I've never broached the subject in class," says a professor.

Yet that year, 700 people reach out to the Guidance and Counselling Services of Université de Montréal, even though the tragedy had only 300 direct and indirect witnesses. The rapid response of the service, which held a first meeting with 125 witnesses on Friday, December 8, is considered a model in the report of the De Coster Taskforce, which, in 1991, reviewed the interventions around the Polytechnique tragedy.

But the students want to turn the page, "keep going, not be held back by this tragedy, not get sidetracked," psychologist Claude Pratte, director of the Guidance and Counselling Services, explains to Ouimet.[41]

38. Virginie Boulanger, "Avons-nous bien couvert la tragédie de Poly?" [Did we cover the Polytechnique tragedy well?], op. cit. (my translation).
39. Michèle Ouimet, "Un décembre 90 fébrile à cause des examens" [A restless December 1990 because of the exams], *La Presse*, December 1, 1990 (my translation).
40. Michèle Ouimet, "Les étudiants parlent: les médias se sont payé un 'party' avec Poly" [Students talk: media had a 'field trip' with Polytechnique], *La Presse*, December 1, 1990 (my translation).
41. Ibid.

Years later, some will say that the Polytechnique leadership didn't encourage a commemoration of the events, at least not for as long as the cohorts who lived through them were there.

In fact, the memory of the massacre was immediately erased. Within three days, the classrooms were painted a new color, the stained carpets were changed, and the bullet holes in the walls were plugged. Few traces remain when the students come back to Polytechnique on Friday, December 8 to pick up their personal belongings. When the school reopens for good the following Monday, everything is gone.

Too fast? But how else could we have done it? That's what the former President of Polytechnique Roland Doré, who was a member of the Board of Directors then and became its Chair in January 1990, still says to this day.

The night of the massacre, he was in France. Alerted about the tragedy, he and several members of the delegation he was part of immediately came back to Montreal. Doré chaired the crisis committee put in place to, among other things, organize the victims' funerals and the return to class.

"We had to move towards healing, forgetting, remembering," he still believes, thirty years later.[42] The personnel and students were distraught enough, there was no need to add to their trauma by leaving visible traces of the tragedy.

Interim President Louis Courville remains on the frontline for a long time, taking care of students, the injured, and the families of the deceased young women. He accompanies relatives of the victims who want to walk down the school hallways; he welcomes members of the families in his home; he even meets Lépine's mother. "He felt that this woman must have been completely devastated. He was extraordinary," says André Bazergui, who took over the presidency of Polytechnique in early 1990.[43]

42. Interview with Roland Doré, June 17, 2019 (my translation).
43. Interview with André Bazergui, June 17, 2019 (my translation).

Coping with the shock

Support was provided on an individual basis by psychologists and members of the staff, like Courville or professor Jean-Paul Baïlon, who was also described as an important resource. "He was amazing. He was one of the strongest afterwards, and supported many students and faculty members. To get through a crisis like that, you have to focus on the positive and that's what he did. He's an incredible man," insists Doré.[44]

But still, in the end, routine took over, with nothing set up to respond to what many from Polytechnique were experiencing on a day-to-day basis.

Looking back, Nathalie Provost, injured that night, notes that in 1989, there were fewer concerns about mental health.

She, herself, was back at Polytechnique in mid-January 1990. As if nothing had happened. It was the same for one of her injured classmates, France Chrétien. "I had one semester left," she says. "And I wanted to see what it would be like…."[45] To see, in fact, if she was capable of finishing what she had started.

In those days, people didn't talk about steps to follow when you've experienced trauma. "Post-traumatic stress disorder didn't exist back then," says Provost today.[46]

Jacques Duchesneau and André Tessier, both directors of sections of the MUC Police in 1989, who were at Polytechnique that night, agree wholeheartedly. "A lot of police officers suffered psychological consequences, but they were not recorded," says Tessier, who was responsible for the police operation.[47]

At the 25th anniversary of the tragedy, Duchesneau talked about colleagues who had retired or been out on sick leave, haunted by what they could or should have done differently that evening. He too, was asking himself those questions.

He mentioned a colleague who had rushed to the building as soon as he arrived at 5:22 p.m. But he eventually decided to wait for backup. Until

44. Op. cit.
45. Interview with France Chrétien, July 25, 2019 (my translation).
46. Interview with Nathalie Provost, June 19, 2019 (my translation).
47. Interview with André Tessier, April 16, 2019 (my translation).

his death, he "carried the trauma related to this moment of hesitation," said Duchesneau.[48]

Many people involved in the tragedy had a similar reaction. Coroner Paul G. Dionne, who was first to examine the bodies of the young women in the makeshift morgue at Polytechnique, suffered years later from severe PTSD, he confided to *La Presse*.[49]

Jean-Simon Venne, a student who was there on December 6, 1989, said in 2014: "My friends [...] and I were tortured for a long time by the idea that we should have done something [...]. We would go through the sequence of events and identify all the missed opportunities. I understand how soldiers suffering from post-war trauma must feel. To get over that, you have to lock your memories and all your questions in a box in the deepest recess of your memory."[50]

Criminologist Geneviève Parent devoted her Master's thesis to the forgotten victims of the tragedy, the men and women who were injured or saw the gunman. Titled *Polytechnique: neuf ans plus tard, conséquences à long terme d'une hécatombe* (Polytechnique: nine years later, long-term consequences of a hecatomb), it was submitted to Université de Montréal in 1999.[51]

During an interview on the occasion of the 15th anniversary of the tragedy,[52] Parent shared that many of the people she approached refused—sometimes aggressively—to talk to her. As for the people she interviewed, they were living with the physical, psychological, and even social repercussions of the tragedy, all poorly understood by the public. For Parent, this stresses the importance of individualized follow-up, particularly over time, for victims of such tragedies.

This opinion is echoed by one of the Polytechnique survivors. With time, support, and the desire to regain psychological health, it's possible to

48. Patrick Lagacé, "Ce que la police a appris à Poly" [What the police learned at Polytechnique], *La Presse*, December 6, 2014 (my translation).

49. Michèle Ouimet, "Polytechnique vue de l'intérieur, 20 ans après" [Polytechnique seen from the inside, 20 years later], *La Presse*, November 30, 2009.

50. Jean-Simon Venne, "Dossier Rose blanche" [White Rose Special Report], *Poly*, fall 2014, vol. 11, no 3, 12 (my translation).

51. Geneviève Parent, "Polytechnique: neuf ans plus tard, conséquences à long terme d'une hécatombe," Master's thesis (Montreal: University of Montreal, 1999).

52. Mathieu-Robert Sauvé, "Polytechnique: les années n'effacent pas l'horreur" [Polytechnique: years don't erase the horror], *Forum*, December 6, 2004.

overcome the trauma of such a horrific event, believes Asmaa Mansour, severely injured on December 6.[53]

However, some victims didn't make it. After the massacre, a few men committed suicide: a student in the summer of 1990, whose parents also killed themselves later; a relative of one of the victims; the engineering student who worked as a paramedic and helped so many victims on the evening of December 6 ended his life three years later....

Paramedic Louise-Marie Lacombe, who knew him, told Radio-Canada: "It might not have been the only cause, but we can't ignore the trauma it inflicted on those who were inside and couldn't do anything."[54]

Some students delay their return to Polytechnique, others pursue their engineering studies elsewhere or change fields altogether. None of these disrupted life journeys have been recorded. Nor were the ways in which everyone tried to pull through while remaining at Polytechnique.

At the time, "we couldn't afford to fall apart," says Guy Brunelle, the employee who hid students under the false floor in the server room.[55] But after..."I had nightmares for over two years," he recalls with emotion. "When I would go to bed at night, as soon as I closed my eyes, I would hear it...."

A psychologist friend explained that this was a normal process after such a tragedy, so he waited for time to do its job. He's also convinced that jogging, a regular practice, helped him pull through. And he continued to work, happy that the Polytechnique leadership had erased the bullet holes, bloodstains, and other traces of the massacre so quickly.

But still, it takes years to recover from such a tragedy, he adds. Noises that sound like detonations can make him jump, and watching films where people kill each other left and right, no thank you.

But he never felt like telling his story. He has never discussed the event with his colleagues.

A restraint shared by others, like Normand Gaboury, a former Polytechnique student who was there on December 6 and tried to help the victims. Post-tragedy analyses by people from the outside deeply irritated him. He explains it this way during an interview with *Le Devoir*, on the

53. Interview with Asmaa Mansour, July 5, 2019.
54. Myriam Fimbry, "Polytechnique, témoignage" [Polytechnique, testimonial], Radio-Canada, November 28, 2014 (my translation).
55. Interview with Guy Brunelle, June 19, 2019 (my translation).

occasion of the 15th anniversary of the massacre: "There were all kinds of pseudo-specialists telling us how we were supposed to feel. There was also a lot of morbid curiosity. The only people I felt comfortable with, to talk about it or not talk about it, were the people who were there that night."[56]

"If we needed comfort and to talk about it, it would happen between us," says engineer Brigitte Saint-Pierre that same year. She too, was at Polytechnique on December 6, 1989, just a few steps away from the last classroom where Lépine hit.[57]

Men and women together

The idea of solidarity comes up in all the student testimonials, from the day after the tragedy up to this day.

There were so many expressions of support in December 1989 that "we covered the walls of the top floor of Polytechnique, from floor to ceiling, with them. Our 115th graduating class came out of this trying event extraordinarily close," remembered Jean-Simon Venne, a board member of AEP in 1989, at the 25th anniversary of the tragedy.[58]

And women are particularly conscious about not ignoring the role that the men played.

Thirty years later, Asmaa Mansour still considers that we don't talk enough about the actions that the men took to help those who were injured.[59]

She mentions the student who saved her life by pushing her to the ground when, already hit by two bullets, she was frozen in front of Lépine. And another who took a bullet in the neck that was destined for her.... The students who helped the victims did so while risking their lives, insists Mansour. Indeed, with the speed at which the events took place, who could have realized that Lépine was only targeting women?

56. Clairandrée Cauchy, "Le chant du cygne" [Swan Song], Le Devoir, December 4, 2004 (my translation).
57. Brigitte St-Pierre, "J'étais alors en deuxième année de Poly" ["I was in my second year at Polytechnique then"], Le Devoir, December 10, 2004 (my translation).
58. Op. cit.
59. Op. cit.

The men-women divide present in the public debate has always been strongly rejected by the Polytechnique student community. In 1991, it becomes the subject of *Au-delà du 6 décembre*, a short documentary by young filmmaker Catherine Fol, herself an alumna of Polytechnique.

Nathalie Provost is at the center of it. She rejects critiques faulting her for telling Lépine that Polytechnique students were not feminists. She also insists on the deep sense of equality between men and women that pervades the school. Studying in a non-traditional field, she says she doesn't need anyone to lecture her. Plus, you don't develop a sophisticated argument when you have a weapon pointed at you; you just want to save your life.

The film revives the polemic....

Yet on the ground, at the start of the school year in 1990, 214 female students are enrolled compared to 122 six years earlier. In total, they represent 16% of enrolled students—compared to 11% in 1984—or 860 female students out of a student body of 5,400 spread over every level from bachelor's to doctorate.

But compared to many other schools, Polytechnique remains a male world. At the time, 56% of the student population of Université de Montréal is female, and schools that used to be primarily male, like law and medicine, now count approximately 60% female students.

Nonetheless, change is happening in engineering too. As part of a series of articles on the first anniversary of the Polytechnique tragedy, journalist Michèle Ouimet interviews first-year students. She writes: "They had decided a long time ago to go to École Polytechnique and the tragedy of December 6 didn't affect their decision at all. Except for one of them, Line. 'I was encouraged,' she explains. 'If women had decided to not go into engineering because of crazy men like Marc Lépine, it wouldn't have been right.'"[60]

60. Michèle Ouimet, "Un décembre 90 fébrile" [A restless December 1990...], op. cit.

Flowers offered in homage to
the victims on the campus of
École Polytechnique.

Because They Were Women

LESSONS LEARNED FROM THE TRAGEDY

Investigations are initiated to understand the gaps in the different interventions that took place on December 6, 1989.

First, at the end of January 1990, Alain St-Germain, Chief of the MUC Police, presents the results of an internal investigation to the executive committee of the Montreal Urban Community, and acknowledges the gaps that fall within his purview.

Then, a study on security at École Polytechnique, begun several months earlier, is submitted to the institution in January 1990. The gaps identified are such that the institution is described as being full of holes.

Teresa Z. Sourour's report, submitted in May 1990, is even more specific: her dispassionate description identifies several shortcomings. In fact, if Marc Lépine hadn't committed suicide, he could have continued his carnage unimpeded—particularly since he had sixty more bullets on him, as the Coroner points out. She writes: "Thank God, he decided by himself that it was enough."

Her report concludes with a long list of questions addressed to all the services that participated in the intervention of December 6, 1989. Implicated are the 911 Call Centre, Urgences-santé, the MUC Police, and the Security Services of Université de Montréal and École Polytechnique.

To answer these questions, in the summer of 1990, the Quebec government sets up a task force chaired by Robert De Coster, a career administrator in the public sector. De Coster works with five people: two doctors, an engineer, an attorney, and a nurse specializing in psychosocial interventions. Their mandate is to study the role and functioning of all the services involved in the tragedy.

At the end of March 1991, they present an exhaustive report: 415 pages, without the appendices, listing 141 recommendations. It's uncompromising, as summarized in a *Le Devoir* article: "Taking no prisoners, the report goes after the monolithic and autocratic management of the MUC Police; the indifference of the government around emergency care [...]; the heads of École Polytechnique, who neglect the security of their students to preserve their institution's autonomy [...]. And they are unforgiving towards Urgences-santé whose effectiveness is 'zero.'"[61]

The lesson is harsh, but it will be learned.

Polytechnique rapidly invests in the training of its security guards and modernizes its security system by installing security guard stations at the building's main entrances, as well as video cameras, and new locks...It also sets up an emergency number and creates a plan that allows first responders to find their way through the school more easily.

911 modifies their system so incoming calls are immediately geolocated; no need to look up an address in order to send help anymore.

At the MUC Police, now the SPVM (Service de police de la Ville de Montréal), December 6, 1989 was a real turning point. Now when there's a shooting, officers don't wait; they rush to neutralize the shooter to make him understand that he's not in control, and to protect people who haven't been hit yet.

And none of this is improvised. "Many new courses were created to train officers in conducting high-risk interventions," explains André Tessier, who was the Director of the Crimes against Persons section during the Polytechnique massacre and, in that position, was responsible for the police operation.[62]

This approach, which is constantly being improved upon, has proved successful, particularly during the shootings at Concordia University in 1992 and Dawson College in 2006, where, despite the intentions of the shooters, the number of killings was contained. Jacques Duchesneau, who became MUC's Chief of police in 1994, adds the example of the attack on Parliament in Ottawa in October 2014. The Security Services immediately intervened; there was an exchange of gunfire and the shooter was killed.

Now, in active shooting situations, the speed of the response takes priority.

61. Josée Boileau, "Polytechnique: le rapport de Coster écorche Urgences-santé et la police de la CUM" [Polytechnique: Coster's report bruises Urgences-santé and the MUC Police], *Le Devoir*, March 28, 1991 (my translation).
62. Interview with André Tessier, April 16, 2019 (my translation).

After, 1992–2019

VIOLENCE AGAINST WOMEN
BECOMES A PUBLIC ISSUE

A POSITIVE OUTCOME of the Polytechnique massacre and the debate that followed is that it took violence against women out of the private sphere where it had previously been confined. It became a public issue whose importance was finally recognized, as a group of researchers noted: "After the event where fourteen young women lost their lives, research centers on family violence and violence against women were created throughout Canada. The National Day of Remembrance and Action on Violence Against Women [on December 6] was instituted by the Parliament of Canada in 1991."[1]

In Quebec, female researchers come together under the Centre de recherche interdisciplinaire sur la violence familiale et la violence faite aux femmes (The Interdisciplinary Research Center on Family Violence and Violence against Women). Inaugurated in 1992, the Centre is affiliated with Université de Montréal, Université Laval, and McGill University, in collaboration with the group Relais-femmes and Fédération des CLSC du Québec.

Relatives of the victims of the massacre also rapidly founded the Fondation des victimes du 6 décembre contre la violence in order to support organizations working on this issue. In addition, for years the

---

1. Joannie Leclerc, Geneviève Malboeuf, Yannicka Poirier and France Gagnon (ed.), "L'action gouvernementale en matière de violence conjugale: entre équité et égalité," *PolÉthicas*, September 24, 2017 (my translation).

Fondation organized the commemoration of December 6, presenting a concert each time.

At the 15th anniversary of the tragedy, the first president of the Fondation, Suzanne Laplante-Edward, mother of Anne-Marie Edward, who was killed that evening, tells *Le Devoir* that the tragedy really raised awareness: "Before, women would die one by one and it was reported in the newspapers, that's all. Now, there's a lot more sensitivity."[2]

For its part, immediately after the attack at Polytechnique and every year since, the Collectif masculin contre le sexisme has been compiling a list of women killed by men—and most of them are victims of a spouse, an ex-boyfriend, or a sexual partner.

This issue is also taken seriously at the governmental level.

In June 1991, in Ottawa, a parliamentary committee submits a report with the explicit title: *La guerre faite aux femmes* (The war against women). It leads to the creation, by Brian Mulroney's government, of the Canadian Panel on Violence Against Women. The group, co-chaired by Québécoise Marthe Asselin-Vaillancourt, travels to 139 locations in all corners of Canada, meeting 4,000 people, 84% of them women. Their efforts also result in nearly 700 position papers and some twenty studies about specific aspects of the problem.

The final report is published in June 1993 under the title *Changing the Landscape: Ending Violence—Achieving Equality.*[3] It lists over 400 recommendations, but is nonetheless disappointing. For feminist groups, not surprised by the findings, it's too broad and lacks a specific timetable. Conversely, commentators will only focus on a few numbers, distorting and making fun of them.

However, the report exposes the scope and multiple aspects of the problem, confirmed by a study by Statistics Canada, also conducted in 1993, and made public in November.

Some 12,300 women are interviewed as part of the study. The results are eloquent: 51% of Canadian women aged sixteen or older have been victim of physical or sexual violence and, in the vast majority of cases, they

2. Clairandrée Cauchy, "Le chant du cygne" [Swan song], *Le Devoir*, December 4, 2004 (my translation).
3. Canadian Panel on Violence Against Women, *Changing the Landscape: Ending Violence—Achieving Equality; Final report*, Ottawa, 1993.

knew their aggressor. In addition, 25% of women have been victim of violence from a current or former spouse.

Yet, these shocking numbers don't silence critics. As researcher Solange Cantin, an expert on domestic violence, writes:

> These results were received with consternation but were generally not contested when they came out because of the credibility of Statistics Canada. However, while it was hoped that this data would put an end to the debate on numbers, some people questioned which acts in this investigation were considered violent and claimed that Statistics Canada was exaggerating. […] Since it was difficult to object to the numbers, the debate on the nature and scope of the violence shifted to a question of definition.[4]

This debate over semantics will only amplify.

However, the topic is now part of the zeitgeist, transcending the borders of Quebec and Canada. Also in 1993, the UN General Assembly adopts the Declaration on the Elimination of Violence against Women, officially recognizing the problem for the first time. It's followed in 1999 by the inauguration of the International Day for the Elimination of Violence against Women, set on November 25.

In Quebec, 1993 is also a year of action. Pressured by the Regroupement québécois des centres d'aide et de lutte contre les agressions à caractère sexuel (RQCALACS), in operation since 1979, Quebec's Health and Social Services Minister, Marc-Yvan Côté, puts in place the Groupe de travail sur les agressions à caractère sexuel. The group is chaired by Diane Lemieux, coordinator of RQCALACS, and submits its report in 1995. It will influence the government's future direction.

4. Solange Cantin, "Les controverses suscitées par la définition et la mesure de la violence envers les femmes," *Service social*, vol. 44, no 2, 1995, 29 (my translation).

Still in Quebec, a specific form of violence against women is brought to the forefront: violence within couples. In 1993, the organization Quebec Native Women creates a committee on domestic violence and conducts a study on the subject. More generally, after extensive consultation, a domestic violence intervention policy is adopted by the Quebec government on December 6, 1995.

It is more comprehensive than the Politique d'aide aux femmes violentées, adopted by Quebec in the mid-1980s to support organizations working in this field and to facilitate the police and legal handling of these cases.

With the 1995 policy, "a unified vision of the problem is implemented and ministries combine their actions."[5] There's recognition that this type of violence rests on the aggressor's assertion of power and control over his victim, and that this is a violation of the fundamental rights of women. The Politique is accompanied by an action plan that will be updated several times, no matter which government is in power.

But the masculinist movement is experiencing rapid growth and it strongly opposes this new tool:

> Starting in the mid-1990s, a few opponents try to make their points-of-view heard through the media. They denounce the sexism and injustices they are being subjected to. They recognize the existence of domestic violence, but question how feminists define it within the realm of politics [...]. While data from the Minister of Public Security confirms that women are a majority among victims of offences committed in a domestic context, groups of opponents lobby for a greater recognition of male victims. These opponents will be active from 2004 to 2012 [...].[6]

5. Gagnon et al., op. cit., 4.
6. Ibid., 4–5

The rise of masculinism

This reaction is part of a wave of antifeminism, whose voices are strong, and even violent.

In the year after the events of Polytechnique, men will lay claim to Marc Lépine. On March 8, 1990, a student at the Cégep de Valleyfield even tries to replicate the attack. He carries a switchblade and a gun that he points at four female students in his class. The teacher, Johanne Soucy-Proulx, manages to calm him down.[7]

Similar incidents take place in universities in Kingston, Toronto, and Vancouver. On the first anniversary of the Polytechnique tragedy, a man is arrested on the doorstep of the Notre-Dame Basilica where a commemorative ceremony is taking place. He's hiding an ice pick in his sleeve and carrying Lépine's list of victims.

For French historian Christine Bard, specialist in women's history and co-editor of *Antiféminismes et masculinismes d'hier et d'aujourd'hui*,[8] it's clear that Lépine is the "pioneer of masculinist terrorism," appearing at the moment when new means of communication are facilitating the dissemination of hate speech.[9] Harassment becomes easier.

In the fall of 2005, a man is found guilty of making death threats to FFQ. In his e-mails, he calls himself "the reincarnation of Marc Lépine."[10] In 2009, UQAM increases security around a conference marking the 20th anniversary of the Polytechnique massacre because of virulent rhetoric on certain blogs, one of which makes a hero of Lépine. No direct threats but "it's better to be ready for everything," explains the person responsible for University Security Services.[11]

7. Bruno Bisson, "Un étudiant armé menace de tuer en pleine classe" [An armed student threatens to kill in the middle of a class], *La Presse*, March 9, 1990; André Cédilot, "La personnalité de la semaine: Johanne Soucy-Proulx" [Personality of the week: Johanne Soucy-Proulx], *La Presse*, March 18, 1990.

8. Christine Bard, Mélissa Blais and Francis Dupuis-Déri (ed.), *Antiféminismes et masculinismes d'hier et d'aujourd'hui*, (Paris: Presses universitaires de France, 2019).

9. Stéphane Baillargeon, "Antiféminismes et masculinismes d'hier et d'aujourd'hui: des salauds manifestes" [Antifeminism and masculism of yesterday and today: manifest bastards], *Le Devoir*, May 18, 2019.

10. Christiane Desjardins, "Il voulait 'finir le travail de Marc Lépine'" [He wanted to "finish" Marc Lépine's job], *La Presse*, November 22, 2005 (my translation).

11. Amélie Daoust-Boisvert, "Polytechnique, 20 ans après—Un attentat contre le féminisme" [Polytechnique, 20 years later—An attack against feminism], *Le Devoir*, December 5, 2009.

Marking that anniversary, the newspaper *Le Soleil* dedicates a series of articles to masculinist groups, who are in the media spotlight. The spectacular actions of Fathers 4 Justice members—such as climbing the Mount Royal Cross and the Jacques-Cartier bridge in 2005, and holding a twenty-six-hour siege perched at the top of a billboard at the entrance of the same bridge, blocking traffic again, in 2006—draw a lot of attention.

Manon Monastesse, Director of the Fédération de ressources d'hébergement pour femmes violentées et en difficulté du Québec, a federation of shelters for women fleeing abuse, notes the impact of this activism: "I feel the escalation, the discourse is making its way into public consciousness. I'm in the media about fifty times a year and this year, I've noticed that the first question journalists ask has to do with the e-mails received from these groups."[12]

The discourse is accompanied by actions. Shelters receive multiple access to information requests, by masculinist groups and must devote precious time and energy to answering them. And the term "feminazi" starts to circulate.

One of the arguments put forward by masculinists is that women too, are violent. Analysts will have to use every argument to nuance this perception. A study by the Institut de la statistique du Québec (ISQ), published in 2003 and titled *La violence conjugale envers les hommes et les femmes, au Québec et au Canada, 1999* (Domestic violence towards men and women, in Quebec and Canada, 1999) devotes itself to it.[13]

Of course, the phenomenon of violence is complex—both genders can be aggressors. But, as *Le Devoir* points out in an editorial about the ISQ study,

> past a certain point, nuances become irrelevant. For example, the worst attack primarily reported by men assaulted by their spouse involves the woman hitting or biting them. Women, on the other hand, report being forced into unwanted sexual activities or their spouse trying to strangle them.

12. Valérie Gaudreau, "Les antiféministes toujours bien présents" [Antifeminists still very present], *Le Soleil*, December 5, 2009 (my translation).

13. Denis Laroche, *La violence conjugale envers les hommes et les femmes, au Québec et au Canada, 1999*, coll. Conditions de vie (Québec: Institut de la statistique du Québec, 2003).

The study indicates that we need to distinguish between situational violence (a screaming match that gets out of control) and marital terrorism. In the latter—characterized by control of the other person, harassment, and severe violence—women are the targets.[14]

Governmental and legal institutions increasingly take into account these types of explanations, refining their approach to violence against women.

For example, in the 1999 case *R v Ewanchuk*, the Supreme Court clearly rejects the presumption of implied consent, which is often use as defense in cases of sexual assaults. Consent must be voluntary, communicated, and continuous. To think otherwise is to promote myths and stereotypes, Judge Claire L'Heureux-Dubé forcefully declares.

In another example, the *Civil Code of Quebec* is amended in 2006 to allow the termination of a lease in cases of domestic violence or sexual assault.

However, authorities are not always up to expectations. The omnipresence of violence affecting Indigenous women is a good example. Despite the numbers and repeated requests, Stephen Harper's Conservative government refuses to set up an investigation into murdered and missing Indigenous women. The leader of the Liberal Party, Justin Trudeau, will promise to do so—a promise that he will keep once elected in 2015. But no one knows what happened to the thick report submitted by the commissioners in the spring of 2019, which concludes it is genocide.

A new awareness

In everyday life, however, women have become particularly sensitive to the question of violence against them. Québécoises participate in huge numbers in the social media campaigns #AgressionNonDénoncée in 2014—originally created in English as #BeenRapedNeverReported by journalists Sue Montgomery from Montreal and Antonia Zerbisias from Toronto—and

14. Josée Boileau, "6 décembre" [December 6], *Le Devoir*, December 6, 2003 (my translation).

Because They Were Women

Le Collectif 8 mars—which represents more than 700,000 women throughout Quebec—demonstrates in front of the Montreal Courthouse at the beginning of Gilbert Rozon's trial, on March 8, 2019.

Demonstration by the movement Ensemble, brisons le silence (Together, let's break the silence) denouncing harassment and sexual assaults faced in everyday life, on October 29, 2017.

#MoiAussi in the fall of 2017, in the wake of the #MeToo movement launched in the US, and quickly gone global.

These public testimonials lead to the creation, in the fall of 2016, of the movement Québec contre les violences sexuelles, to report assaults on university campuses, and the campaign #EtMaintenant, which, in January 2018, encourages Québécoises to build on the momentum started by #MoiAussi.

This leads to concrete results. In Quebec, the Act to Prevent and Fight Sexual Violence in Higher Education Institutions is adopted in 2017.

In 2015, the number of sexual assaults reported to the police across Canada starts to go up. At the end of 2017, the increase is so significant that Statistics Canada links it explicitly to the #MoiAussiMeToo movement. This momentum continues all through 2018, according to the organization that compiles annual data on criminality. This shows a real change of perspective on the part of the victims, especially since "the quasi-totality of the reported assaults were classified as Level 1, meaning that they involved no weapon and left no apparent physical injuries."[15] Whether critics like it or not, the battle of definitions is over—even if sexual assault remains one of the least reported crimes.

What's more, people become aware of the difficulty for victims of assault to navigate the justice system: few press charges, even fewer follow through, and many who do are harmed by the system.

In December 2018, Parti Québécois Quebec National Assembly member Véronique Hivon decides to take up the fight; the system has to adapt to victims, not the other way around. She is heard by the new Coalition Avenir Québec (CAQ) government, which comes into power in October. In March 2019, surrounded by representatives of all parties, including Hivon, Minister of Justice Sonia Lebel announces the creation of a committee of experts whose mandate is to find ways to improve the processing of judicial and extra-judicial cases of sexual assault. The report is expected in 2020.

15. Stéphane Marin, "Les agressions sexuelles dénoncées en hausse" [Reported sexual assaults are increasing], *La Presse canadienne*, July 22, 2019 (my translation).

FEMINISM REGAINS
ITS STRENGTH

Stopped in their tracks at a moment they thought the momentum would last—"the wind in their sails," as columnist Francine Pelletier later wrote to describe the "obvious" progress made in 1989 that "could only keep going"[16]—militant feminists manage to get moving again after the Polytechnique tragedy, and not only to fight violence against women.

Their demands highlight new issues and sometimes lead to legislative changes. The movement itself sees the creation of new approaches, new groups, and new alliances. At the individual level, women don't go back home; instead, they continue to carve their paths within male strongholds.

Abortion

In 1990, the feminist movement thought it had lost the great battle for the right to abortion with the introduction of Bill C-43 in the House of Commons, which recriminalized it. But on January 31, 1991, the Bill is defeated in the Senate after a free vote. However, the battle is narrowly won: forty-three for and forty-three against. But the Senate rules stipulate that in case of a tie, a bill must be rejected....

From then on, opponents of abortion modify their strategy. Conservative MPs start to introduce motions or private bills in the House of Commons. To this day, there have been some forty attempts, to no avail; no government wants to reopen the debate. In fact, in April 2012, the National Assembly of Quebec calls directly on Conservative Prime Minister Stephen Harper to calm his troops: the unanimous motion asks "the federal government and the Prime Minister of Canada to end the lingering ambiguity relative [to the right to abortion]" (my translation).

Along the same lines, the Supreme Court renders new decisions maintaining that a fetus is not a person, and so doesn't have legal rights.

---

16. Francine Pelletier, "Je me souviens" [I remember], *La Vie en rose*, Hors-série, 2005, 34 (my translation).

In this context, although vigilance is still called for given the strong anti-abortion lobby, we should worry less today about a new ban than about limited access to abortion and the abortion pill (offered in Canada only since 2017, after fifty-seven countries authorized it, including the US in 2000, and France, which pioneered it, in 1988).

New gains, new cases

But there's no shortage of cases to defend. Laws adjust as best they can, as these few examples show:

- After a first pilot project involving midwives in 1990, a first birth center opens its doors, still as a pilot project, in Gatineau in 1994. The practice is finally legalized in 1999 and an undergraduate program in midwifery is immediately created at Université du Québec à Trois-Rivières. In 2004, mothers obtain the right to give birth at home with a midwife.

- In 1990, the federal government establishes, through employment insurance, a paid ten-week parental leave, which can be taken by the mother or father. In 2001, paid parental leave increases to thirty-five weeks. Starting in 2006, maternity and parental leaves are now managed entirely by Quebec, which makes it possible for the province to improve them. The Quebec parental insurance plan is now extended to self-employed workers and includes a five-week paid paternity leave.

- Automatic deduction of child support payments is put in place in 1995.

- The *Pay Equity Act*, applicable to businesses of ten employees or more, is adopted in 1996 and goes into effect in November 1997.

- In 1997, the new Ministry of Families oversees the creation of a network of subsidized early childhood centers, in addition to establishing mandatory full-time kindergarten.

- In 2001, employment equity programs are implemented in public and non-governmental institutions of a hundred employees or more.

Parity is also on the agenda. In politics, Groupe Femmes, Politique et Démocratie has been advocating for it since 2005. Premier Jean Charest makes an important symbolic gesture in 2007 when, for the first time in Quebec, he appoints a ministerial cabinet in which gender parity is observed. In addition, as part of the *Act Respecting the Governance of State-Owned Enterprises*, he makes it a requirement for their boards of directors to comprise an equal number of men and women.

The cultural realm sees the creation of the group Réalisatrices équitables in 2007, and of the movements Femmes pour l'équité en théâtre in 2016, and Femmes en musique in 2017. The latter fiercely claims its place in the numerous music festivals in Quebec, where women are far from being equally represented, when they're not entirely missing.

Important women in the history of Quebec are finally incorporated in the public space:

- Jeanne Mance is officially recognized as co-founder of Montreal (2012).

- A monument dedicated to women in politics, representing Idola Saint-Jean, Marie Lacoste-Gérin-Lajoie, Thérèse Forget-Casgrain, and Marie-Claire Kirkland[17] is unveiled in front of the National Assembly in Quebec City (2012).

- Prix Marie-Andrée-Bertrand for social innovation becomes the second of fourteen Prix du Québec to be named after a woman, after Prix Denise-Pelletier (2012).

- Marie-Claire Kirkland is the first Québécoise to receive a national funeral (2016).

17. As a politician in the 1960s, she was known as Claire Kirkland-Casgrain.

Unveiling of the monument paying tribute to pioneering women in politics on December 5, 2012.

Gérin-Lajoie

Idola St-Jean

Thérèse Forget-Casgrain

oste Gérin-Lajoie, Idola St-Jean et Thérèse
nnières qui ont lutté pour le droit de vote e
s au Québec, obtenu en 1940.

Ensemble elles ont pavé la voie à Marie-Claire
Kirkland qui devint, en 1961, la première femme
élue à l'Assemblée législative du Québec.

Marie-Claire Kirkland

Spectacular actions

Militant feminists also hold major gatherings, marking the return of a collective force that's not satisfied with individual progress, but rather intends to take a political and global view on the status of women.

A first step is taken in that direction in May 1992. Over a thousand feminists participate in a three-day forum in Montreal, organized by FFQ under the theme "Un Québec féminin pluriel pour un projet féministe de société" (A Quebec feminine plural for a feminist vision of society).

It's a year of major changes at the head of FFQ. The leadership is renewed. Françoise David, a seasoned militant, becomes vice-president. She takes over the presidency in 1994. During her tenure, which will last until 2001, the organization "morphs into an extraordinary social network, a central hub for the mobilization of women in Quebec and elsewhere."[18] And it attracts political and media attention.

At the time, FFQ was in the thrall of a leadership and personnel crisis. Upon taking the helm, David refocuses the Fédération's priorities to concentrate on women's poverty. She proposes to orchestrate a spectacular action. This becomes the march Du pain et des roses (bread and roses), which travels through Quebec from May 26 to June 4, 1995.

The march is a huge success, both in terms of participation and public support, and calls for a response from the government. It's followed by the Marche mondiale des femmes (World march of women), still under the aegis of FFQ, held in 2000 and annually thereafter. Each time it brings together women from nearly one hundred countries.

Attracted by this renewal, FFQ's member groups increase in number from seventy-one in 1992 to one hundred forty-four in 1996. That year, the allied member status is created. Even l'Association féminine d'éducation et d'action sociale, which is not generally associated with militant feminism, signs up, which allows it to participate in the activities of FFQ.

David's commitment to inclusion, her credibility among the general population, and the new life breathed into the movement democratize the

18. Flavie Trudel, "L'engagement des femmes en politique au Québec: histoire de la Fédération des femmes du Québec de 1966 à nos jours," PhD diss. (Université du Québec à Montréal: 2009).

Françoise David,
President of
Fédération des
femmes du
Québec (FFQ).

"feminist" label previously rejected by so many women. It's no longer necessary to be a militant to be a feminist!

Added to this is the increased presence of women in the workplace, thanks to greater education for girls, and to measures adopted to facilitate work and family life balance.

– ✳ –

Now that they're workers, many women realize that the equality they experienced in school doesn't translate into the workplace—and even less so when they're in the minority.

From stupid or obscene jokes to the obligation to work harder to prove that they "deserve" their position, without forgetting the old boys' clubs constantly regenerating themselves, and the glass ceiling insidiously blocking the advancement of competent employees who would be happy to become "second women" after the pioneers…the examples abound. Nothing is a given yet.

The march Du pain et des roses, held from May 26 to June 4, 1995.

Facing phenomena like harassment, misconduct, cyberbullying starting as early as in high school, love stories gone wrong…feminism becomes a uniting term. So much so that if a female minister refuses the label, particularly if she's responsible for the Status of Women as will be the case with Lise Thériault in 2016, no one understands.

The polarization of the 1980s is gone. An anecdote from 1989, inconceivable today, demonstrates it.

On Monday, December 11, 1989, there's a huge crowd at the Notre-Dame Basilica: 5,000 people have come to pay tribute to the victims of Polytechnique. A journalist from *La Presse* approaches a few people in order to gather testimonials for his article. A woman talks to him and identifies herself using the first and last name of her husband. A young woman overhears her and says: "You must have a first name, Madam, everyone has a first name."[19] The older woman feels criticized, while the young one finds her old-fashioned…Two worlds exist side by side. Thirty years later, what

Homage to pioneer trade-unionist Léa Roback during the march Du pain et des roses.

19. Richard Fortin, "Une foule recueillie offre son appui aux parents accablés" [A crowd in mourning offers its support to the overwhelmed parents], *La Presse*, December 12, 1989 (my translation).

prompted this skirmish seems from another time. Unity has been achieved between women: they now exist fully and on their own.

Moreover, activism is back on the agenda of new generations of engaged women.

In 2003, 2,000 young feminists under thirty gather in Montreal for an event organized by FFQ themed "S'unir pour être rebelles" (Uniting to be rebels). Ten years later, in Montreal again, FFQ holds the Forum des États généraux de l'action et l'analyse féministes (Forum about the general state of feminist action and analysis), which was preceded by two years of gatherings held everywhere in Quebec. There will be some 800 participants.

This activism takes new approaches. The specific problems faced by certain groups of women—Indigenous, lesbian, disabled, from cultural or racial minorities...—take more and more room, shaking older feminist organizations and giving rise to new ones. This leads to heated and sometimes wrenching debates, causing the movement to become split between different schools of thought.

National funerals for the victims of Polytechnique on December 11, 1989.

But the word "feminism" is no longer something Quebec women run away from.

NATHALIE PROVOST, FEMINIST

In December 1989, Nathalie Provost becomes the face of young women who refuse the feminist label, and she is widely criticized for it. In Catherine Fol's film, *Au-delà du 6 décembre*, broadcast in 1991, she expresses her exasperation, throwing the book *Polytechnique, 6 décembre*, which she had started leafing through in front of the camera, far away from her.

Three years later, in 1994, it's a calm young woman working as an engineer that Francine Pelletier, now a reporter at CBC, interviews for a news story on the occasion of the fifth anniversary of the tragedy. It's a thrilling television moment.

When the journalist asks what Marc Lépine represents for her, Nathalie answers:

– A poor guy…

– That's all? insists the journalist.

Nathalie doesn't answer but nods her head 'yes.'

– And what did you represent for him? asks Pelletier.

– You.

– Me?

– Uh-huh! says the young woman, nodding with a smile.

– You? repeats the journalist.

Nathalie, playful, is amused at Pelletier's response.

– Yes, you, Francine Pelletier, Lise Payette, Janette Bertrand! I was a symbol of you. I was easier to take, to find out.

– You must be angry at me, then? says the journalist.

– Not at all! Nathalie immediately replies.

She says she now realizes that a woman studying engineering may very well be the equivalent of a militant feminist....

Nathalie will continue to refine her thinking on this issue, as shown in many of the interviews she later gives.

She's particularly eloquent in the student paper *Le Polyscope* in 2014:

"When I was a girl, feminism was what militant women did in the 1940s, 1950s, 1960s, 1970s.... For me, Lise Payette was a feminist. She was among the first wave of women who fought for what they wanted.

"I wasn't the first female student at Polytechnique—there had been several before me. So, when I got there, it felt like the fight to carve a place for women had already taken place. [...] When I told Marc Lépine that I wasn't a feminist, I was telling those women that they are so much more than how I saw myself. I had it easy, the door was already open so I couldn't take this beautiful title and claim it for myself. It was later that I understood I have to claim it because if I don't, I'm not recognizing the value of what those women did before me."[20]

20. Camille Chaudron, "Vingt-cinq ans plus tard avec Nathalie Provost" [Twenty-five years later with Nathalie Provost], *Le Polyscope*, November 28, 2014.

EVEN MORE "FIRST WOMEN"

1997 Suzanne Blanchet, President and CEO of Cascades Tissue Group, first woman at the head of a paper mill in North America.

1998 Linda Goupil, first woman Minister of Justice in Quebec.

1998 Monique Gagnon-Tremblay, first woman Leader of the Official Opposition.

1992 Jocelyne Gros-Louis, first woman elected Grand Chief of the Huron-Wendat First Nation of Wendake.

1993 Monique Gagnon-Tremblay, first woman Minister of Finance in the Quebec government.

1999 Julie Payette, first Quebec woman astronaut in space.

1994 Raymonde Verreault, first woman Chief Justice in Quebec, at the Municipal Court of Montreal.

2002 Francine Ruest-Jutras, first woman President of Union des municipalités du Québec.

1995 Louise Gagnon-Gaudreau, first woman and first civilian to be Director General of the Institut de police du Québec.

2002 Claudette Carbonneau, first woman President of Confédération des syndicats nationaux.

1997 Chantale Patenaude, first woman General Director of the Quebec Prospectors Association.

2002 **Louise Harel**, first woman Leader of the National Assembly.

 2011 **Diane Lemieux**, first woman CEO of the Commission de la construction du Québec.

2003 **Françoise Bertrand**, first woman President of the Quebec Federation of Chambers of Commerce.

2012 **Pauline Marois**, first woman Premier of Quebec (and the only Premier to have been the target of an attack, on the night of her election. The shooting incident results in one dead and one injured).

2004 **Diane Lemieux**, first woman House Leader at the National Assembly.

2013 **Michèle Thibodeau-DeGuire**, first woman Chair of the Board of La Corporation de l'École Polytechnique de Montréal (after being the first woman to graduate from the university Polytechnique in Civil Engineering in 1963).

 2007 **Pauline Marois**, first woman leader of a party represented in the National Assembly, with Parti Québécois.

 2008 **Monique Leroux**, first woman at the head of a Canadian financial institution as Chair of the Board and CEO of Mouvement Desjardins.

2014 **Diane Francoeur**, first woman President of the Fédération des médecins spécialistes du Québec.

Among others...

2011 **Nicole Duval Hesler**, first woman Chief Justice of the Quebec Court of Appeal.

AT POLYTECHNIQUE...

Marc Lépine had no impact on the enrollment of female students at Polytechnique. They are there in September 1990, and there will be more and more of them in the following years, in percentage as well as in total numbers, going from approximately 860 at the time to 2,500 in 2019.[21]

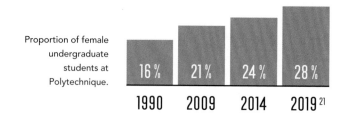

Proportion of female undergraduate students at Polytechnique.

16 % — 1990
21 % — 2009
24 % — 2014
28 % — 2019 [21]

The proportion of female students at Polytechnique is greater than at other engineering schools in Quebec (17%) and Canada (18%). Their number vary according to the program; all levels combined, they're in majority in biomedical and chemical engineering, equal in geological and industrial engineering, and in minority (15% or less) in computer, software, and mineral engineering. In addition, 28.5% of students in civil engineering and 18.4% in mechanical engineering are female.[22]

The number of female professors has also increased. The first woman professor is hired in 1967. In 1999, 7% of professors at Polytechnique are women. Today, they represent 15% of the faculty, or forty-three professors.

We also see improvement with practicing engineers. L'Ordre des ingénieurs du Québec (OIQ) included only 4.3% women in 1989–1990, compared to 11% in 2009 and 15%—out of 64,500 members—in 2018.

21. As of September 23, 2019.
22. Polytechnique Montréal, institutional data.

Supporting the next generation of women

Women are still in the minority in the engineering world, but not for a lack of encouragement to take up that field.

In February 1990, the Canadian Committee on Women in Engineering is created, bringing together representatives of both genders from universities, associations, and businesses. It is chaired by Monique Frize, the first woman to receive a diploma in engineering from the University of Ottawa in 1966. In her final report, Frize notes that the committee was created in response to the Polytechnique massacre: this "catalytic event gave our investigation great impetus."[23]

Over a period of two years, the committee holds a national forum, six public forums across Canada, and conducts extensive research.

Several testimonials are shared with the committee, describing uncomfortable situations, mostly unacknowledged until then. Frize comes to this realization: "As I heard the experiences of other women, I began to remember incidents of harassment and discrimination, the public insults and private apologies. This personal recovery from amnesia made it easier for me to understand the 'denial' which is so prevalent among female engineering students and young women engineers who are just beginning their careers. Like many others, I had been so busy advancing my career that I had not taken time to recognize the negative behavior and attitudes of some of my male colleagues."[24]

In 1992, in addition to the sometimes enthusiastic but often disturbing personal stories, the report from the committee "includes twenty-nine recommendations that marked a turning point in the evolution of women in engineering. These recommendations suggested avenues to fight stereotypes discouraging the participation of women in engineering from a young age, as well as in universities, the workplace, and professional associations."[25]

23. Canadian Committee on Women in Engineering, *More than just numbers*, April 1992.

24. Ibid., Foreword by Monique Frize.

25. Anne Roy, Donatille Mujawamariya, Louise Lafortune (ed.), *Des actions pédagogiques pour guider des filles et des femmes en STIM (Sciences, Technos, Ingénierie et Maths)* (Québec: Presses de l'Université du Québec, 2014) (my translation).

In 2011, the initiative begun twenty years earlier is revisited as part of a two-day gathering in Ottawa. "Twenty-five new recommendations emerged, each accompanied by a 'course of action' to reach the proposed goals, and a list of individuals and public authorities most susceptible to turn these goals into reality."[26]

This work will lead to concrete results. In 2015, Engineers Canada, which brings together the twelve provincial and territorial associations that supervise the practice of engineering, launches the initiative 30 by 30, which aims to have women represent 30% of engineers in Canada in 2030. Since then, engineering schools have been putting various measures in place to achieve this goal.

For Kathy Baig, President of OIQ, the Polytechnique tragedy changed everything: "It sent a clear message that women want to stay in the profession," and this is as obvious for men in the field as it is for women, she specifies.[27]

As a result, more attention is paid to the obstacles faced by women in non-traditional fields. "Polytechnique is particularly progressive in that regard," says professor Caroline Boudoux in the special edition that *Poly*, the magazine of the university, dedicated to the 25th anniversary of the massacre.

Symbolically, since September 2018, Canada has a School of Engineering associated with a woman: the Gina Cody School of Engineering and Computer Science at Concordia University in Montreal. The school was named to honor the first PhD student in Building Engineering at Concordia, Gina Parvaneh Cody, who graduated in 1989. Cody also donated fifteen million dollars to Concordia to support scholarships, research chairs, and a fund focused on equity and diversity.

26. Ibid.
27. Interview with Kathy Baig, July 17, 2019 (my translation).

Measures to support female engineering students in Quebec

- 1996: The Ministry of Education creates the contest Chapeau, les filles! (Hats off to you!) to encourage female students in high school-level vocational training and college-level technical training who aspire to go into traditionally male jobs. In 2001, a university component, Excelle Science (Excellence in Science), is added for female students in science or engineering.

- 1998: École Polytechnique establishes the Marianne-Mareschal Chair, whose mandate until the end of 2016 is to promote engineering to women through workshops, mentorships, conferences, etc. The Poly-FI committee has since taken over, while the Poly-L committee promotes gender equity in engineering.

- 1999: The program Les filles et les sciences: un duo électrisant, which means "Girls and sciences: an electrifying duo" is launched, giving teenage girls aged thirteen to fifteen the opportunity to learn about engineering through workshops organized at Polytechnique and École de technologie supérieure (ETS).

- 2014: For the 25th anniversary of the tragedy, Polytechnique creates the Order of the White Rose scholarship, which carries an award of $30,000 given annually to a Canadian female student in engineering who wishes to pursue a Master's or a PhD in Canada or somewhere else in the world. The institution also launches the Week of the White Rose, an annual fundraising campaign that supports the participation of girls from disadvantaged communities to Folie Technique—a science camp at Polytechnique created in 1991.

- 2019: ETS launches the Objectif Féminin pluriel campaign.

- 2019: OIQ launches Le Programme des ambassadrices (The Ambassador program), through which female engineers meet with teenage girls in high schools and cégeps in their region.

Added to this list are another twenty or so scholarships offered by private businesses, OIQ, and the Fonds des victimes du 6 décembre 1989, to support engineering students.

Gun control

The other big problem that the Polytechnique community decides to take on—gun control—is a lot more controversial. It launches less than a week after the massacre.

In 1989, professor Michel Rigaud was teaching in the Department of Metallurgical Engineering. On December 6, several of his female students died. Like many of his colleagues, he immediately felt the need to take action, and what was most urgent to him was clear: limiting access to the kind of firearms Marc Lépine used. Supported by AEP, he starts a petition, which he writes with Daniel Leblanc, another professor.

On the 25th anniversary of the tragedy, Rigaud writes:

> I remember the very cold day of December 15 [1989], when my wife and I were going up and down Saint-Denis Street [in Montreal] to collect signatures from passers-by. For me, who had never been an activist, it was a strange experience. [...] The favorable response was like a balm on our wound.[28]

The public's interest encourages the petitioners to solicit support from personalities and companies. "One of our good shots was to convince Royal Bank of Canada to post our petition in its branches," says Rigaud.[29]

In 1990, President of AEP Alain Perreault presents a petition with over 560,000 names to the then federal Minister of Justice Kim Campbell, who goes to École Polytechnique to take receipt of it.

The following year, the Coalition for Gun Control is created under the direction of Heidi Rathjen, a Polytechnique student who was present during the shooting, and Wendy Cukier, a professor at Ryerson Polytechnic in Toronto. Rathjen becomes director general of the coalition.

She manages to bring together over three hundred organizations (police corps, women's organizations, public health organizations, unions, etc.) to pressure the federal government in order to obtain a tightening of gun control regulation and to establish a gun registry.

It's the beginning of a long saga.

On February 26, 2010, a few days before International Women's Day, Heidi Rathjen, co-founder of the Coalition for Gun Control, and Thierry St-Cyr, member of the Bloc Québécois, sound the alarm to save the gun registry.

28. Michel Rigaud, "Dossier Rose blanche" [White Rose Special Report], *Poly*, Fall 2014, vol. 11, no 3, 11.
29. Ibid.

The steps of the battle

- 1991: Bill C-17 is passed in Ottawa. The bill tightens the process of firearm acquisition (increased background check measures; mandatory safety training; new definitions of restricted and prohibited firearms, etc.).

- 1995: Bill C-68 is passed. *The Firearms Act* requires anyone who owns a firearm or buys ammunition to have a permit and most of all, it provides for the registration of all firearms in a registry before January 1, 2003. This registry is a huge victory for the Coalition for Gun Control, which allows Heidi Rathjen to leave her post.

- 2006: Stephen Harper's Conservative government—a minority government—is elected in Ottawa. In June, a first bill to end the mandatory registering of long-guns is introduced, but it dies on the order paper.

- 2007: New governmental attempt to get rid of the registration of long-guns. Once again, the bill dies on the order paper.

- 2008: *The Anastasia Act*, named after eighteen-year-old Anastasia De Sousa, killed in the Dawson College shooting in Montreal on September 13, 2006, enters into force in Quebec. Adopted in 2007, the *Act to Protect Persons with Regard to Activities Involving Firearms* bans the possession of firearms in educational institutions, as well as in public and school transportation. It also requires health professionals to report dangerous patients. Restricted firearm owners must be members of a shooting club and train at least once a year.

- 2009: PolySeSouvient is created. It brings together Polytechnique student and alumni associations, former presidents of these associations, witnesses, survivors, and family members of the victims of the December 6, 1989 massacre. The movement intends to protest the dismantling of the firearm registry envisaged in Ottawa. Heidi Rathjen, co-founder of the movement, becomes the coordinator.

- 2011: In May, the Conservatives are re-elected in the federal elections but this time, they form a majority government. In October, Harper's government introduces Bill C-19, which provides for the abolition of the firearm registry. In December, the government of Quebec announces that it will seek a legal remedy to save the province's registry data.

- 2012: Bill C-19 is passed. *The Ending the Long-Gun Registry Act* goes into effect in April. The government of Quebec immediately obtains an injunction from the Superior Court that prevents the destruction of the province's registry data and maintains the obligation to register firearms for Quebec users. The legal debate lasts all year, which saves the province's data, while in October, all other records from the federal registry have already been destroyed.

- 2015: The debate about the registry goes to the Supreme Court. In March, the court renders its judgment and rejects both Quebec's application for unconstitutionality and the transfer of Quebec's records. In June, Bill C-42, introduced in the House of Commons in October 2014, is passed and goes into effect. *The Common Sense Firearms Licensing Act* simplifies the permit system, but strengthens the rules in case of infractions related to family violence. In December, in Quebec, Philippe Couillard's Liberal government introduces Bill 64 to create a Quebec registry.

- 2016: In June, Bill 64 is adopted at the National Assembly by ninety-nine votes against eight. The *Firearms Registration Act* goes into effect at the end of January 2018.

- 2017: The federal government, now Liberal since the 2015 elections, indicates that it won't recreate the long-gun registry, but that Quebec can repatriate data that concerns it. Trudeau's government also modifies the composition of the Canadian Firearms Advisory Committee (CFAC) to include representatives of the public health sector, women's organizations, the movement for gun control, and so on.

- 2018: In March, Bill C-71 is introduced in Ottawa. The bill reinstates certain measures abolished by the Conservatives, including the obligation for gun dealers to record all sales of firearms in a register. The Act to amend certain Acts and Regulations in relation to firearms receives royal assent in June 2019.

- 2019: In May, Quebec Minister of Public Security, Geneviève Guilbault, in office since the election of the CAQ government in the fall of 2018, introduces Bill 25, which modifies the *Firearms Registration Act* to ease certain bureaucratic requirements. In July, Nathalie Provost, vice-president of CFAC, survivor of the Polytechnique massacre, and spokesperson for PolySeSouvient, resigns from the federal committee, denouncing in her resignation letter "the inaction of (or little action taken by) the Liberal government around gun control."[30]

PolySeSouvient is active in all these debates and often backed by other organizations, including OIQ and ETS.

Opponents

Opponents are also very active. Since 2012, they've been gathered under the collective Tous contre un registre québécois des armes à feu, which means "All against a Quebec firearms registry." Claude Colgan, brother of one of the Polytechnique victims, Hélène Colgan, is a member. In line with the collective, he doubts the effectiveness of a registry. In their writing and in interviews, members of the collective specify that, to prevent massacres, we should offer more support to people who suffer from psychological distress. And they add that if someone present at Polytechnique on December 6, 1989 had known how to use a firearm, Lépine could have been stopped before he killed fourteen victims.

In fact, some hunters not only oppose a tightening of the rules around firearms, but they reject any connection to the events of December 6, 1989. "Every year, they bring it up again to try to draw a few tears from us," says a hunter from Plessisville in a *Le Devoir* article about the Quebec long-gun registry.[31]

30. Jim Bronskill, "Une survivante de la tuerie de Polytechnique quitte le comité sur les armes à feu" [A survivor of the Polytechnique massacre resigns from the Firearms Advisory Committee], *La Presse canadienne*, July 15, 2019 (my translation).
31. Marco Bélair-Cirino and Dave Noël, "Le massacre qui hante le Québec" [The massacre haunting Quebec], *Le Devoir*, February 6, 2016 (my translation).

Moreover, the nomination of Nathalie Provost to the vice-presidency of CFAC was strongly denounced by the Canadian Coalition for Firearm Rights that, in 2018, filed a formal complaint about her with the Commissioner of Lobbying of Canada. Provost is also the target of virulent personal attacks—just like female columnists who support the firearm registry. They are more violently targeted than their male colleagues who hold the same opinion.

As Marie-Claude Lortie writes on the occasion of the 25th anniversary of the Polytechnique tragedy: "Gun lovers [...] are under the impression that I want to rip their souls out when I talk about gun control. There are also very angry men who insult me and think that Quebec is led by women who are dead set against them."[32]

HOW TO REMEMBER...

December 6, 1989 affected a lot of people: direct witnesses, of course, and all those who lived through the horror of that night—families, college personnel, police officers, medical teams, journalists.... And the spectators of the tragedy, glued to their television.

Added to them are the women that Lépine listed with the intention of killing them—a list that he was carrying in his pocket during the massacre. And other women too, anonymous, left out of history, but who were profoundly touched, as shown by this scene described by blogger Patrick Bellerose:

> I was nine years old on the morning of December 7, 1989, the day after the Polytechnique tragedy. [...] My own personal tragedy, in the head of a nine-year-old kid, was unfolding in the kitchen. My mother, bent over the ironing board, a pile of clothes next to her, seemed absolutely shaken.

32. Marie-Claude Lortie, "25 ans après Poly" [25 years after Polytechnique], *La Presse*, December 6, 2014 (my translation).

Of course, there was the tragic death of the fourteen young women. [...] But there was more. My mother seemed hurt in her core. Personally affected. Back then, I thought it was empathy for the parents of the victims. [...] Now I know that on that day, she saw her certainties crumble. An entire life punctuated by important victories for women and the counter had just been reset.[33]

There are thousands more of these stories throughout Quebec. But this tragedy, rich in images and emotions, experienced both in the public sphere and the intimacy of one's life, doesn't seem to resonate much in the cultural world.

The contrast is great when we look at other moments that have shaken Quebec society, such as the 1970 October Crisis or the 2012 Maple Spring, both of which are invoked either directly or in the subtext of plays, films, and novels....

The case of the 2012 Maple Spring is particularly striking. The student protests, clashes with the police, and marches punctuated by the banging of pots were immediately featured in, or used as background for, many narratives penned by young Québécois novelists, who were marked by this moment. And it continues to be a source of inspiration.

Lépine's act also destabilized the student populations of the time. They discovered that universities were not immune to violence in general, and violence against women was revealing itself in all of its horror. But, the young writers of the 1990s didn't use this fact in their works.

Moreover, as actor-playwright Gilbert Turp, who wrote the play *Pur chaos du désir*, which addresses December 6, 1989, explains: "The Polytechnique massacre is a historical event. In fact, it's the most significant event of political violence in the history of Quebec, if we don't count the Patriots in 1837. It's bigger than the October Crisis or the Oka Crisis, if only in terms of the number of people killed."[34]

---

33. Patrick Bellerose, "Un 7 décembre sur Terre" [A 7ᵗʰ of December on Earth], *Huffington Post*, December 5, 2014 (my translation).

34. Christian St-Pierre, "Gilbert Turp et la tragédie de Polytechnique: scènes de la vie conjugale" [Gilbert Turp and the Polytechnique tragedy: scenes from married life], *Voir*, January 8, 2009 (my translation).

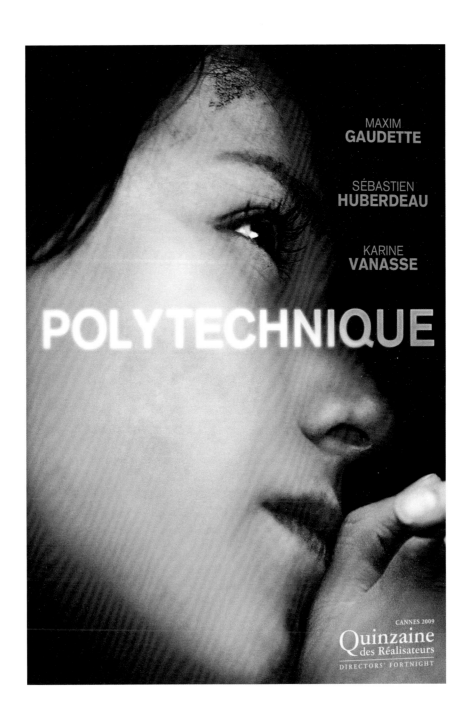

MAXIM
GAUDETTE

SÉBASTIEN
HUBERDEAU

KARINE
VANASSE

POLYTECHNIQUE

CANNES 2009
Quinzaine
des Réalisateurs
DIRECTORS' FORTNIGHT

The fear of forgetting has often been mentioned over the years by people who lived through the tragedy. In 2003, an editorial covering the anniversary in *Le Devoir* noted it at the outset: "From year to year, December 6 requires more effort. What was it again? Oh yes, the Polytechnique killings!"[35]

Even at the 25th anniversary, this fear is present. Louis Courville, Interim President of Polytechnique at the time of the tragedy, echoes the sentiment: "We have to collect the testimonials of hundreds of people to have a record while it still exists. Maybe some of it is trivial, but it's too early to tell. When historians study texts, details can open up our understanding of the story."[36]

And yet, despite the many possible avenues for inspiration, only a few works talk about Polytechnique, and they appear years after the tragedy.

Among them, the film *Polytechnique*, a project of actress Karine Vanasse, directed by filmmaker Denis Villeneuve, is notable. Released in February 2009, it takes on the delicate task of recreating the tragedy on screen, but with a respectful approach that resists the trap of sensationalism. This translates, among other things, into the use of black and white. The film is widely hailed and now serves as a history lesson for all those who were not born at the time.

Plays also address the tragedy:

- *The Anorak* by Adam Kelly Morton (2002), a monologue that follows Marc Lépine's journey and delivers a theatrical punch: men and women spectators are separated and the actor, author of the piece, addresses exclusively the men until the scene of the massacre.

- *Nicole, c'est moi* by Pol Pelletier (2004), a reworking of the play *Cérémonie d'adieu* by the dramaturge and actress, which she initially created to commemorate the 10th anniversary of Polytechnique, and then

35. Josée Boileau, "6 décembre" [December 6], *Le Devoir*, December 6, 2003 (my translation).
36. Isabelle Paré, "La peur de l'oubli" [The fear of forgetting], *Le Devoir*, December 6, 2014 (my translation).

transformed into a feminist rereading of world history, culminating on December 6, 1989.

- *Forêts* by Wajdi Mouawad (2006), inspired by the Polytechnique massacre, a young Québécoise's search for identity leading to the discovery of what she owes to women with tragic fates.

- *14 Abeille*, a first play by Québécoise and French authors Anne Pépin and Emmanuelle Favier (2007), which revisits the horror of the massacre through fourteen mythical figures of female power (Isis, Elisabeth I, la Corriveau…) using video and sound.

- *The December Man* by Colleen Murphy (2007), where a young male student at Polytechnique tries to cope with the fact that he escapes the massacre but finally kills himself. The play received the 2007 Governor General's Award for English-language drama and was performed across Canada and in London, England.

- *Pur chaos du désir* by Gilbert Turp (2009), the breakdown of an academic couple in the aftermath of the massacre, with the story beginning on the evening of December 6, 1989 and ending a year later.[37]

In terms of books, while essays, academic articles, and articles penned by militant feminists have explored the different aspects of the tragedy—several are mentioned in this book—works of fiction have been more rare:

- *Leçons de Venise* by Denise Desautels (Éditions du Noroît, 1990), a book of poetry written immediately after the massacre. Inspired by a Michel Goulet sculpture where books are perched atop rifles, the author draws a link between those weapons and violence against women.

- *The Dead of Winter* by Lisa Appignanesi (McArthur & Company, 1999), a detective novel where a famous actress, haunted by the Polytechnique tragedy, is found hanged in a cottage in the Laurentides.

37. Gilbert Turp explains his approach for this play, which he started writing over a dozen years before it was produced: "Around me, a lot of couples were separating. As if men and women were at war with each other. I think that Polytechnique caused new animosity between the sexes."—Paul Journet, "Pur chaos du désir: l'amour après Polytechnique" [Pure chaos of desire: love after Polytechnique], *La Presse*, January 24, 2009 (my translation).

- *Dans l'ombre de Marc Lépine* by Luc Labbé (Amerik Média, 2008), a novel in which the main character, a young engineer who knew Lépine in cégep, questions his responsibility in the tragedy (Luc Labbé, who was a student at Polytechnique in 1989, came across the shooter a few minutes before the start of the massacre).

- *Sel et sang de la mémoire* by Élaine Audet (Sisyphe, 2009), a collection of poems that recall the death of the fourteen students, one of which, Geneviève Bergeron, was a friend of the author's daughter.

- *Soudoyer Dieu* by Thérèse Lamartine (JCL, 2009), features a young woman named Renée-Pier, whose best friend was killed at Polytechnique and who, from then on, questions all aspects of male-female relationships.

- *L'homme qui haïssait les femmes* by French author Élise Fontenaille (Grasset, 2011), where, under the guise of writing fiction (the male character's name is Gabriel Lacroix), the author paints a portrait of the killer and of a Quebec that rapidly went from the oppression of Catholicism to feminism.

Pol Pelletier during a performance of *Nicole, c'est moi.*

In addition, four novels published in 2019 allude to the deadly shooting of December 6, but within a broader narrative. This is something new.

- In *Lockdown* by Guillaume Bourque (Leméac), the Polytechnique massacre is one of several current events in Quebec that the author integrates into the life of his characters.

- In *Sale temps pour les émotifs* by Jean-François Beauchemin (Québec Amérique), the first of 145 short stories, titled "Beauté perdue" (Lost beauty), features Florence Madeleine Syers from the UK, the first woman World Figure Skating Champion in 1908. Her ghost will look over the fourteen young women killed at Polytechnique.

Forêts by Wadji Mouawad, presented during the Festival TransAmériques (FTA).

- In *Le patron* by Hugo Meunier (Stanké), the author imagines a new past for Lépine, one of the many characters in this thick novel, which takes place in 1989 and today; the Polytechnique massacre is one of the narrative's driving force.

- In "L'apparition du chevreuil" by Élise Turcotte (Alto), the main character, a female author, denounces the hateful discourses of men referring to the Polytechnique massacre.

In terms of memoirs, we can find:

- *6 décembre. De la tragédie à l'espoir: les coulisses du combat pour le contrôle des armes* by Heidi Rathjen and Charles Montpetit (Libre Expression, 1999).
- *Poly 1989: témoin de l'horreur* by Adrian Cernea (Lescop, 1999), where the professor who was in the first classroom Lépine entered recounts his experience.
- *Vivre* by Harold Gagné (Libre Expression, 2008), where the journalist interviews Monique Lépine, mother of Marc Lépine.

The commemorations

Every December 6 since 1989, Polytechnique commemorates the tragedy, but soberly, mindful of showing respect to the relatives of the victims.

Unrelated to the institution, other commemoration events have sprung up, organized as much by the families as by various groups of women. The question of what meaning to give the massacre is on the agenda for a long time.

Which is why 2014 is an important date: the 25th anniversary of the tragedy will be the commemoration of healing. A genuine moment for coming together that inscribes the event in the collective memory and, above all, publicly recognizes the massacre as an antifeminist act that reflects what exists in society, "exceptional representation of a terribly ordinary reality: the prevalence of violence against women and misogyny."[38]

38. Josée Boileau, "6 décembre, 14 femmes, 25 ans" [6th of December, 14 women, 25 years], *Le Devoir*, December 6, 2014 (my translation).

During the official ceremony held at the Mount Royal Chalet, this analysis, contested for so long, reaches consensus. The Mayor of Montreal Denis Coderre, in particular, says: "We have evolved; this tragedy from twenty-five years ago has opened our eyes on the hundreds and thousands of small tragedies that happen to women every day [...], but the battle hasn't been won yet."[39]

The December 6, 1989 massacre has been marked every year with:

- A wreath of white roses laid in front of the Polytechnique commemorative plaque by representatives of the institution and of student associations.

- Marches and discussions about violence against women, held mostly by feminist and labor groups, in Montreal as well as in the rest of Canada, and also in France.

- Minutes of silence in the Parliaments of Quebec and Ottawa.

- Ceremonies of remembrance and concerts, long organized by the Fondation des victimes du 6 décembre contre la violence. From 1991 to 1999, the concerts were performed by Orchestre métropolitain of Montreal, directed by Agnes Grossmann and broadcast live by CBC and Radio-Canada radio.

- Demonstrations by the Coalition for Gun Control, then by PolySeSouvient during the height of the battle to obtain, then save, the firearms registry.

Throughout the years and across the entire country, various events were added to these recurring gestures:

39. Amarilys Proulx, "25 ans plus tard, le Québec pleure encore les victimes" [25 years later, Quebec still mourns the victims], *Agence QMI*, December 6, 2014.

1st anniversary (1990):

- A *memorial service* at the Notre-Dame Basilica, organized in collaboration with Polytechnique and AEP. A marble plaque engraved with the names of the fourteen victims is unveiled and hung on the southwest wall of the building. Several churches ring their bells at 5:00 p.m.

- A *vigil* organized by groups of women in front of Polytechnique.

- A *roundtable* at Université de Montréal with, among others, Violette Trépanier, Minister Responsible for the Status of Women; Alain Saint-Germain, Chief of the MUC Police; and Léa Cousineau, Chair of the executive committee of the City of Montreal. The panelists have to answer questions prepared by the organizers of the event, who come from RQCALACS, L'R des centres de femmes du Québec, and Regroupement provincial des maisons d'hébergement et de transition pour femmes victimes de violence conjugale. Some three hundred people attend the discussion.

- *Elsewhere in Canada*, the House of Commons pays homage to the victims, the University of Calgary creates a *scholarship* for a student in a non-traditional field, and a *commemorative monument* is unveiled in Toronto, among other things.

Vigil organized by women's organizations in front of Polytechnique on December 6, 1990.

2nd anniversary (1991):

- The inauguration by the federal government of December 6 as *National Day of Remembrance and Action on Violence Against Women.*

- The creation by Jack Layton,[40] Michael Kaufman, and Ronald Sluser from Ontario of the *White Ribbon Campaign* to protest against men's violence against women. A white scarf was worn by female engineers during the collective funerals of the victims and other ceremonies in December 1989. The white ribbon has since become a symbol of the Polytechnique massacre in all of Canada.

- A *torchlight procession* to Église Saint-Jean-Baptiste in Montreal, where the Metropolitan Orchestra, conducted by Agnès Grossmann, presents a tribute concert to the victims.

- A *meeting* between a coalition of feminist groups, with Françoise David and Diane Lemieux as spokespersons, and Quebec Premier Robert Bourassa, to pressure him to launch an awareness campaign on violence against women.

3rd anniversary (1992):

- The *unveiling* of the monument *Enclave*, which pays tribute to the assassinated women, in Minto Park in downtown Ottawa. From then on, the monument becomes a gathering place to commemorate the anniversary of the Polytechnique massacre.

- In Vancouver, Agnes Grossmann directed the Vancouver Symphony Orchestra and its Choir in a memorial *concert.*

4th anniversary (1993):

- At the end of a commemoration ceremony, the 715 students of Collège de Montréal, all men, form a *peace sign* for women.

40. Jack Layton is then a City Councilor in Toronto. He becomes Leader of the New Democratic Party in 2003.

5th anniversary (1994):

- The *publication* in all of the daily newspapers in Quebec of *Plus jamais* (Never again), a commemorative text written by the Council on the Status of Women, and signed by dozens of organizations and personalities, including Quebec Premier Jacques Parizeau.

- The awarding of three *scholarships* to female PhD students of both Polytechnique and the Department of Physics by the Syndicat général des professeurs et professeures de l'Université de Montréal.

- The filing of a *petition* of 9,000 names with the National Assembly to improve the judicial treatment of cases of women victim of violence.

- The organization of several *activities* in universities and at YWCA Montreal to reflect on violence against women.

- A *torchlight procession* that brings together students from universities and cégeps from across Montreal.

- The memorial *concert* of Orchestre métropolitain with its Choir directed by Agnes Grossmann is broadcast live on CBC and Radio-Canada television....

6th anniversary (1995):

- Quebec Premier Jacques Parizeau presents the new *government policy* to address domestic violence.

7th anniversary (1996):

- The *unveiling* of the sculpture *Memorial*, which depicts 14 bullet holes, by YWCA Montreal. Another monument is dedicated to the victims of Polytechnique in Moncton.

The Canadian flag at the Parliament on December 6, 1999, lowered to half-mast in homage to the victims.

- A *demonstration* by young women who, at 5:00 p.m., block the intersection of Peel and Sainte-Catherine streets in downtown Montreal for fourteen minutes displaying the names of the fourteen women assassinated at Polytechnique.

Monument *Nef pour Quatorze Reines.*

8th anniversary (1997):

• The *unveiling* of a commemorative monument made of fourteen pink granite benches, each inscribed with the name of one of the victims, in downtown Vancouver.

10th anniversary (1999):

• The *unveiling* of the monument *Nef pour Quatorze Reines* by artist Rose-Marie Goulet and landscape architect Marie-Claude Robert at the new Place du 6-décembre-1989, at the corner of Queen Mary Road and Decelles Avenue in Montreal, at the foot of the road leading to Polytechnique.[41]

41. As Claire Roberge, president of the Fondation des victimes du 6 décembre contre la violence, and step-mother of Geneviève Bergeron, one of the fourteen victims, then explained: "We, the families, have often been asked why there was no monument or commemorative place in Montreal when there are so many of them across Canada. [...] Montreal didn't need a monument to remember the tragedy; the scars were huge! But ten years have passed."—Isabelle Hachey, "Parce qu'elles étaient des femmes" [Because they were women], *La Presse*, December 6, 1999 (my translation).

- The memorial *concert* of Orchestre métropolitain with its Choir directed by Agnes Grossmann is broadcast live on CBC and Radio-Canada television.

- Photo *exhibit Un cri un chant des voix* by Diane Trépanière in memory of the victims.

15th anniversary (2004):

- La Fondation des victimes du 6 décembre contre la violence holds a last *commemorative ceremony* and a concert at Église Saint-Jean-Baptiste. FFQ takes over the organization of the commemorative ceremonies starting in 2005.

- The filing of a *petition* of 121,000 signatures by Amnesty International and FFQ with the National Assembly to pressure the government to fund a vast awareness campaign on violence against women.

- *Eleven well-known men*, including Premier Jean Charest, appear in a *photo* by Heidi Hollinger with the heading "La violence contre les femmes, ça nous frappe aussi! Ensemble nous la dénonçons et la combattons." (Violence against women hits us too! Together, we denounce it and fight it).[42]

42. Featured on the photo are: Normand Brathwaite, Claude Béchard, Pierre-Hughes Boisvenu, Philippe Couillard, Boom Desjardins, Jacques Dupuis, Ghislain Picard, Stéphane Quintal, Pierre Reid and Larry Smith.

17th anniversary (2006):

- Louise De Sousa, mother of Anastasia De Sousa, a female student killed on September 13, 2006 in the Dawson College attack, participates in the commemorative *ceremony* organized by FFQ at Place du 6-décembre-1989.

20th anniversary (2009):

- A three-day *international colloquium* brings together 400 women—writers, researchers, politicians, activists—to UQAM under the theme: "La tuerie de l'École Polytechnique 20 ans plus tard—Les violences masculines contre les femmes et les féministes" (École Polytechnique massacre 20 years later—Male violence against women and feminists).

- A *human chain* of 500 people, organized by FFQ at Place Émilie-Gamelin in downtown Montreal shows solidarity with women victim of violence.

- A two-hour private *ceremony* for relatives of the victims and direct witnesses of the tragedy, is organized by Polytechnique at the Notre-Dame Basilica. On this occasion, an honorary doctorate is awarded to Lili-Anna Peresa, the first woman to receive this honor at Polytechnique. A 1987 graduate of Polytechnique, Peresa changed career paths after the tragedy to devote herself to humanitarian causes.

22nd anniversary (2011):

- FFQ *demonstrates* at the entrance of the Montreal Courthouse to bring attention to the difficulty for women victim of violence to obtain justice. The same demonstration takes place at the commemorations of 2012 and 2013.

23rd anniversary (2012):

- Surrounded by six ministers, Quebec Premier Pauline Marois presents the Government Action Plan 2012–2017 on Domestic Violence. Out of the one hundred thirty-five measures, thirty-five concern Indigenous Nations.

25th anniversary (2014):

- A *collective reading* of a message of solidarity titled "C'est à nous tous et toutes de garder la mémoire vivante" on Friday, December 5, takes place at the National Assembly. The text, written by feminist journalist Françoise Guénette, is cut up so that the thirty-one female MPs present, out of a total of thirty-three, can each read a few lines. Several victims of violence against women are mentioned, and particularly the victims of Polytechnique. Rich in emotion, this reading is an exceptional moment in the parliamentary life of Quebec and Canada.

- Several feminist *conferences* are held in the days preceding the anniversary, including at Polytechnique, Université de Montréal, and UQAM.

- The creation at Polytechnique of the *Order of the White Rose* and *Week of the White Rose* to encourage and support the next generation of women in engineering.

- A new showing of the photo *exhibit Un cri un chant des voix* at Maison de la culture Frontenac.

- A *commemorative ceremony* at Place du 6-décembre-1989 organized by the committee 12 Days of Action to End Violence Against Women.

- A *torchlight procession* to the Notre-Dame-des-Neiges Cemetery.

- A *public ceremony* titled "Se souvenir pour elles" (Remembering for them) is held at the Mount-Royal Chalet during which some twenty-five personalities speak, including Quebec Premier Philippe Couillard, Mayor of Montreal Denis Coderre, woman politicians, as well as militant feminists and people who were involved in the tragedy in 1989. To organize this event, an ad hoc committee is formed, bringing together members of the victims' families and Polytechnique representatives, among others.[43]

- At the end of the ceremony on Mount Royal, *fourteen beams of light*, designed by Moment Factory, each representing one of the victims, light up the sky at the exact time the shooting started.

- The concert *En souvenir d'elles* is presented by the Université de Montréal Orchestra.

- The *benefit show Pour elles—Quatorze voix unies*, brings together fourteen well-known performers at Théâtre Outremont, under the direction

43. This ad hoc committee eventually takes the name "Comité Mémoire" and is chaired by Catherine Bergeron, sister of Geneviève Bergeron, who died at Polytechnique. Since 2014, the Comité Mémoire has supervised, in collaboration with the City of Montreal, the annual light beam ceremony on Mount Royal, and is behind the commemoration of the 30th anniversary, which includes this book.

of Lorraine Pintal, in support of PolySeSouvient, which is asking for better gun control.

29th anniversary (2018):

- On September 22, at the request of women ministers of Foreign Affairs gathered in Montreal for a two-day international summit, the Canadian Minister of Foreign Affairs Chrystia Freeland and representatives of families of the victims welcome them to Place du 6-décembre-1989.

Added to these significant events are all the minutes of silence, and all the moments of recollection that discreetly take place every December 6 in myriads of locations. Often because someone—a professor, an activist, a former student of Polytechnique, a police officer who intervened that night, a friend of the victims, or a former boyfriend—vowed to never forget.

THE YOUNG WOMEN

In Memoriam
1989

BARBARA
DAIGNEAULT
GÉNIE MÉCANIQUE

NATHALIE
CROTEAU
GÉNIE MÉCANIQUE

HELENE
COLGAN
GÉNIE MÉCANIQUE

SONIA
PELLETIER
GÉNIE MÉCANIQUE

ANNE-MARIE
LEMAY
GÉNIE MÉCANIQUE

ANNIE
ST-ARNEAULT
GÉNIE MÉCANIQUE

École Polytechnique
de Montréal

GENEVIÈVE
BERGERON
GÉNIE MÉCANIQUE

MARYSE
LAGANIÈRE
EMPLOYÉE DE L'ÉCOLE
POLYTECHNIQUE

MAUD
HAVIERNICK
GÉNIE MÉTALLURGIQUE

MICHÈLE
RICHARD
GÉNIE MÉTALLURGIQUE

ANNIE
TURCOTTE
GÉNIE MÉTALLURGIQUE

ANNE-MARIE
EDWARD
GÉNIE CHIMIQUE

MARYSE
LECLAIR
GÉNIE MÉTALLURGIQUE

BARBARA
KLUCZNIK
WIDAJEWICZ
SC. INFIRMIÈRES
UNIVERSITÉ DE MTL.

"DES ROSES DANS LA NEIGE" (Roses in the snow) is the title of the touching column that distinguished journalist Jean V. Dufresne penned in *Le Devoir* after the Polytechnique tragedy.[1]

The image has stayed to evoke the fourteen young women who were killed. Flowers blown in the wind. Evanescent figures, entwined in the same tragedy, whose premature death and lost youth we grieve. "Sleeping beauties," as they were called twenty-five years later by journalist Shelley Page, who had covered the massacre for *Ottawa Citizen*. At the time, overwhelmed by grief, we didn't see that they were much more. So, Page added: "I should have referred to the buildings they wouldn't design, the machines they wouldn't create, and the products they would never imagine."[2]

Indeed, and talked about the strong women who had carved a place for themselves in a field until then reserved to men, and who felt perfectly comfortable there.

It is these determined women, who stood out in so many ways, that we now need to discover anew.

One by one.

1. Jean V. Dufresne, "Des roses dans la neige" [Roses in the snow], *Le Devoir*, December 8, 1989.
2. Shelley Page, "How I sanitized the feminist outrage over the Montreal massacre," *Ottawa Citizen*, December 6, 2014.

Geneviève Bergeron

THE SURPRISING GENEVIÈVE! The brilliant Geneviève. The endearing Geneviève.

Like her inseparable sister, Catherine, she goes to École FACE, an institution located in downtown Montreal that offers both primary and high school programs, in French and in English. And despite being a public school, it is entirely dedicated to the arts.

Catherine, known as Catou, summarizes the spirit of the place, which persists to this day: "You better be interested in exploring your talents because there, art is all you do: visual arts, music, theatre, choir.... Our talents were developed in that school. And you come out perfectly bilingual."[3]

Geneviève is extremely comfortable in that world; she's talented. And charismatic. "She was beautiful, and she fascinated guys," says Catou about "Gene," who was two years older than her. A *star*.

She seems to be heading for a career as a clarinettist or a singer, two disciplines she excels in. But no, not at all. It will be the sciences instead, and more specifically, engineering.

3. Interview with Catherine Bergeron, June 27, 2019 (my translation).

"In high school, she's simply good at everything: math, chemistry, physics, French. She gets 90% and 100% in everything." It's easy for her, yes, but she also strives for high grades and needs to succeed.

These achievements can open a lot of doors, so Geneviève has to consider all her options. Finally, she explains to her sister: "I'll always be able to play music. So, I should go into engineering; it's a more secure field."

Geneviève enrolls in sciences at Collège de Bois-de-Boulogne. For the first time in their school career, the two sisters attend different institutions. But sports still brings them together—especially basketball games, which they're crazy about.

Then, Geneviève is accepted at Polytechnique. Initially, she's interested in civil engineering but the following year, she switches to mechanical engineering. Her father, Gilles Bergeron, a talented, self-taught architect who is missing a diploma in order to fully achieve his professional potential, is extremely proud.

Her mother, Thérèse Daviau, well-known by Montrealers, is extremely proud too. She's part of the coalition of militants who, in 1974, founded the Rassemblement des citoyens de Montréal to defeat Mayor Jean Drapeau, who was ruling without opposition. She runs for city office and

Geneviève (left) and Catherine with their mother, Thérèse Daviau, in October 1986, during the municipal campaign when she was elected councilor in the district of Plateau-Mont-Royal in Montreal.

ends up city councilor, with two other women, at twenty-eight. She then studies law, becomes an attorney, and goes back to politics in 1986.

For whoever wishes to tear down barriers impeding the advancement of women, Thérèse is an inspiration. It would never occur to Geneviève, or to her family, to think that a woman doesn't have her place in the male world of Polytechnique. Quite the opposite.

Geneviève and her stepfather, René Giroux, in the family home.

So, it's December 1989. Geneviève is twenty-one. She shares an apartment with her best friend, Myriam. She likes her studies; she works hard. She's still the cheerful woman with whom everyone spontaneously wants to be friends. And as her father often tells her: the world is hers.

After December 6

When the Montreal City Council convenes at 6:00 p.m. on the evening of December 6, news has been circulating for a few minutes in the media. There has been an attack, or a hostage-taking, at Polytechnique. Thérèse can't help it; she steps out of the room to call home and make sure that everything is okay. Not really, says Catherine. There are rumors of a massacre at Polytechnique.

Thérèse immediately goes home. When she arrives, a lot of people are already there, and the phone is ringing off the hook. Geneviève has many friends and they all want to know if she's okay…. They're invited to join the family in the big house on Laurier Avenue.

So, everyone is waiting for the beloved Gene, and they talk about her, about this woman whose work is always rewarded with success. Dread increases as time passes. Geneviève has always been careful not to worry people around her—it seems unthinkable she wouldn't get in touch….

Geneviève (right) with her childhood friend, Myriam. In 1989, they were roommates.

Then Catherine talks on the phone with Marco, Geneviève's teammate, who was with her that day. He's vague, simply says that he lost track of his friend. What else can he say to a family sick with worry when he has no information himself?

Hours later, Thérèse's spouse, René Giroux, goes to Polytechnique with a friend of Catherine's. They're redirected to a room in the main pavilion of Université de Montréal. Later, they're invited to go back to Polytechnique, where a makeshift morgue has been set up. That's where Geneviève is….

For the family, the pain is immense. It's the kind of pain that makes you crawl into a ball, that cuts your legs from under you, that breaks your heart.

When she heard about her daughter's death, Thérèse stayed very calm. But later, she'll say that this murder profoundly changed her: "I've always loved life. People used to call me a ray of sun, the life of the party. But after the tragedy, I could feel that something was dead in me. A light went out."[4]

However, she's a woman of action and a feminist. Something positive has to come out of this massacre. Lépine cannot—must not—win. She decides to get involved in combatting violence against women and gun control in Canada.

With other members of the families affected by the Polytechnique massacre, she creates the Fondation des victimes du 6 décembre contre la violence, which, for fifteen years, orchestrates the commemorations of the event, including, in 1999, the inauguration of the monument *Nef pour Quatorze Reines* at Place du 6-décembre-1989. Thérèse remains active with the foundation until her death in 2002.

Claire Roberge, the spouse of Geneviève's father, so Geneviève's stepmother, is also deeply involved with the Fondation, including as a president. "My sister's death really brought our family together, which had come apart after my parents' divorce in the mid-1970s. After the tragedy, we all rallied,"[5] says Catherine.

She will get involved too. Not immediately because at nineteen, it's hard to see your illusions about equality go up in smoke, your protective bubble burst. And to see your big sister, your idol, disappear. Does she realize the loss? "She was beautiful, she was good at everything, and she was so nice. She made each and every one of us feel important! But she wasn't aware of it, so it made us love her even more."[6]

4. Isabelle Hachey, "Les autres victimes de Marc Lépine" [Marc Lépine's other victims], *La Presse*, November 27, 1999 (my translation).

5. Correspondence with Catherine Bergeron, September 8, 2019 (my translation).

6. Correspondence with Catherine Bergeron, September 6, 2019 (my translation).

Through the pain, Catherine grows closer to Marco. For six months after the tragedy, they're inseparable. "He's like a brother to me," says Catherine. "We still see each other to this day."

He eventually tells her in detail about Gene's last moments. Says that he was by her side when they came across the shooter. In fact, they saw him from the back as he was reloading his rifle on the landing of the second floor. And they didn't really understand the scene. "Is this a joke?" Marco wondered. Geneviève reacted right away: "Quick, we have to get out of here!" They went down to the cafeteria. But Lépine went too. They split in order to hide.

Several minutes later, when the police evacuate the place, Marco doesn't know what happened to Gene....

Mourning will be long, but there's so much to do that Catherine jumps into action. Until 2008, she's involved in the fight for gun control, as one of the spokespersons. And she gets back into it again in 2014 as president of the Comité Mémoire, which, since the 25th anniversary event at Mount Royal, commemorates the tragedy every year by illuminating the Montreal sky with beams of light.

Hélène Colgan

HÉLÈNE COLGAN isn't the kind of woman to kid herself. So, when Lépine enters classroom C-230.4, where he's about to begin his massacre, she immediately understands that he's not joking. Because she recognizes his weapon.

Lépine sends the nine women to the back of the class and tells the men to get out. In a corner, Hélène tells her classmates: "Girls, this is serious. He has a .223."[7]

She knows because Claude, her nineteen-year-old brother, is a hunter. But there's no time for more advice, the rest happens so fast…. Hélène dies from a single shot to the head.

The young woman was twenty-three. She was studying mechanical engineering and was completely dedicated to it. No matter whom you ask, the same image keeps coming back: Hélène, deeply immersed in her studies.

She had a good time at Cégep Montmorency. A hard worker in her science classes, she also liked going out to bars, and going dancing. A life like the lives of many people her age.

7. Interview with France Chrétien, July 25, 2019 (my translation).

At university, however, there's a distinct shift. She doesn't go out anymore; she studies. Entirely focused on her classes and very serious about her studies, she has a clear goal: to help the world by becoming an engineer.

But she's still the cheerful woman who caught Diane Gagnon's attention when they met in their second year of high school at Collège Regina Assumpta.

"We quickly became friends," remembers Diane. "What I loved about her was that she was so, so funny. She liked to laugh, she was very dynamic, very cerebral. Yes, she already had an engineer inside her!"[8]

The two women complete each other. Math, chemistry, physics—not for Diane! Hélène has good grades in all subjects but one day, she faces the white page. She has to write a poem for a French class and "it's not her thing," as her friend says. So, they decide to do it together.

"We eventually wrote a short poem about a knife and a fork. We had fun coming up with something like: 'Mister Knife and Madam Fork cross paths to cut food.' It was pretty funny." This was just like Hélène, who would easily get the giggles "and loved putting herself in situations to have fun." But she never wanted to disturb anyone.

In fact, she had the profile of the good student, says Diane today. "Someone who wasn't complicated; not a leader, but not a follower either—just someone who took her place in a group and was liked by everyone. It was easy to communicate with Hélène. She was very nice."

She's always the top of her class. But it's a big deal to get through the program at Polytechnique. The game is suddenly less easy and Hélène decides to give it her all. She perseveres, willing to work hard to reach her goal. She specializes in mechanical engineering. Before she even started at Polytechnique, she had one day floated the idea of building bridges.

The day after the massacre, her father, Clarence Colgan, said: "No one was more studious than her. She worked really hard and read everything she could put her hands on."[9]

8. Interview with Diane Gagnon, July 29, 2019 (my translation).
9. Suzanne Colpron, "Féministe, Hélène Colgan l'était…" [Hélène Colgan sure was a feminist…], *La Presse*, December 8, 1989 (my translation).

Her mother, Liliane, adds that after her undergraduate studies, which she was almost done with, their daughter had plans to do a Master's Degree. She had also received job offers, including one from a company in the region of Toronto. For her mother, Hélène was obviously a feminist. "But she didn't have the word written on her forehead."[10]

After the fall semester of 1989, Hélène was looking forward to a break. She was supposed to go to Mexico for a few days with Nathalie Croteau, her best friend, for a vacation. Their flight was leaving on December 29.

After December 6

The Colgan parents and Claude, their son, hear about the tragedy unfolding at Polytechnique while watching television that night. They try, without success, to get more information. "Around 10:30 p.m., we decided to go," Clarence tells *La Presse* the next day.[11] At Polytechnique, the couple scrutinizes every student coming out of the school, every update of the list of hospitalized students. That's how they figure it out....

"When I met my father's eyes that night, I expected the worst," said Claude to his local newspaper years later.[12]

However, he never participated in the many commemorations that followed. He doesn't agree with the main interpretation of the event and with what he considers an appropriation of the tragedy. He's among those who firmly believe that the use of firearms shouldn't be restricted, and that his sister could have defended herself if she had been armed. He says to *Journal de Chambly*: "Hélène was supposed to take shooting classes a few months before the tragedy."[13]

He has long been an activist with the group Tous contre un registre québécois des armes à feu and he regrets that his deep belief in self-defense,

10. Ibid.
11. Ibid.
12. "26 ans après Polytechnique: Claude Colgan pleure toujours l'assassinat de sa soeur" [26 years after Polytechnique: Clause Colgan still mourns his assassinated sister], *Le Journal de Chambly*, December 4, 2015 (my translation).
13. Ibid.

Hélène and her brother, Claude, with whom she gets along very well.

Hélène (left) at a family Christmas dinner.

with which he associates his sister, has been neglected in analyses of the event.

His perception of the issue is not related to the Polytechnique tragedy, but to an assault he suffered two years earlier, in 1987. He was seventeen, working as a gas station attendant, and found himself with a knife to his throat and two thieves asking for the contents of the cash register.

"For the first time in my life, I understood that whether I was going to live or die was in someone else's hands," he confides in February 2013, at a meeting organized by Tous contre un registre québécois des armes à feu, a report of which can be found on the website of Canada's National Firearms Association.[14] He felt powerless and desperate. The same thing his sister felt....

Hélène during her high school graduation.

14. nfa.ca, testimonial from February 9, 2013, [online] (my translation).

Nathalie Croteau

EVEN WITH GOOD GRADES, it wasn't the norm for teenage girls in the 1980s to think about going into engineering. It put you in a different category; it was proof of a particular kind of determination.

That's why Johanne Truesdell, even thirty years later, says spontaneously and with a lot of emotion in her voice: "There weren't a lot of people like Nathalie!"[15]

They meet at École Secondaire Antoine-Brossard, in Brossard, a Montreal suburb, where Nathalie Croteau lives. She's sociable, enterprising, and very involved—in Brossard, as a member of the Air Cadets, and at school, as part of the organizing committee for the graduation ball, remembers Johanne.

She's very studious and always at the top of her class. She already likes science, which puts her in the "nerds" category, a label that doesn't exactly make you popular. But it doesn't bother her. "She didn't mind," remembers her friend. "When she wanted to do something, she just did it."

In fact, Nathalie is very upfront about what she likes. She gets involved in her school's Génies en herbe group inspired by the popular television

15. Interview with Johanne Truesdell, July 2, 2019 (my translation).

show of the same name, where, every week, the best students from different high schools in Quebec compete against each other.

With this mindset, going to Polytechnique doesn't intimidate her at all, despite the demands of the program and the fact that she finds herself among a small group of women in the middle of a sea of men. She's there to learn: "It was her passion."

Above all, Nathalie is a woman who "is a good listener, has a warm heart, and is always ready to help," says her friend. For her, learning has meaning: she wants to "learn in order to understand, learn in order to accomplish."[16]

Johanne loses track of Nathalie for a time, but bumps into her again at Polytechnique while she's there doing an internship as part of her computer science studies. They set up a time to have lunch together at the cafeteria. They chat about everything, just like they used to do in high school....

In December 1989, Nathalie is twenty-three and she's one semester away from finishing her undergraduate degree in mechanical engineering. After so many years of hard work, she has decided to treat herself. Immediately after Christmas, she's flying to Mexico with other students, including her good friend and classmate Hélène Colgan, for two weeks.

"This would have been her first trip without her family.... It's crazy how things can change with the snap of a finger," observes Johanne with great emotion.

On December 6, Nathalie and Hélène left together but for a very different destination.

16. Correspondence with Johanne Truesdell, September 29, 2019 (my translation).

The young women — Nathalie Croteau

After December 6

Nathalie's family is horrified by the tragedy. Their daughter was killed "all because she was sitting on a chair in a classroom!" exclaimed her father at the time, profoundly shaken by the news.[17] After this first reaction, Nathalie's relatives chose to mourn privately.

In 1993, the City of Brossard decides to give Nathalie Croteau's name to its community center, to pay homage to this deceased citizen who had been so active in her community. The name is kept even after the building is completely rebuilt following a fire in November 2010. The new Centre Communautaire Nathalie-Croteau is inaugurated in September 2015.

And Nathalie's death had a butterfly effect, says Johanne. She decides to get socially involved. For many years, she's on the board of directors of a shelter for women victim of domestic violence, and supports other similar initiatives.

Other friends, especially from their time in high school, are just as moved and decide to become active too. Everyone has the same thought, says Johanne: "Nathalie should never have died this way. It's a huge loss for her family and her relatives, for all of us, for our society. Her death won't be in vain, and we'll take action in her memory as much as we can."[18]

17. "Remembering the Polytechnique victims," *Montreal Gazette*, December 5, 2014. Portraits of the victims drawn from articles published in the newspaper between December 8 and 12, 1989.
18. Correspondence with Johanne Truesdell, September 29, 2019 (my translation).

Barbara Daigneault

OF COURSE, BARBARA DAIGNEAULT gets her first name from Jacques Prévert's famous poem! Her mother loves it so much.[19]

Rappelle-toi Barbara
Il pleuvait sans cesse sur Brest ce jour-là
Et tu marchais souriante
Épanouie ravie ruisselante
Sous la pluie[20]

(Remember Barbara
It was raining non-stop on Brest that day
And you were walking smiling
Content delighted dripping
Under the rain)

Barbara was, indeed, born in a rainy country, in Great Britain, on March 2, 1967. Two years earlier, her father, Pierre-Alain Daigneault, a graduate student in Engineering from Université de Sherbrooke, has been

19. Correspondence with Jean-Christophe Daigneault, September 9, 2019.
20. Jacques Prévert, "Barbara," *Paroles* (Paris: Gallimard, 1946).

awarded the prestigious Athlone-Vanier scholarship, which made it possible for him to go to Birmingham University. So, with his wife, Henriette Therrien, he left for Britain.

The following year, the couple is still abroad but in Bristol, where Pierre-Alain obtains his Master's in Thermodynamics and does an internship in a manufacturer working on the Concorde prototype. This is years before the commissioning of the aircraft in 1976, but it has already entered into myth. Enough to thrill the student!

For her part, Henriette teaches French here and there, becomes pregnant, and gives birth to her daughter at the end of their stay. Barbara arrives in Quebec in the summer of 1967 in her parents' arms. She's four months old. Her brother Jean-Christophe is born in 1969.

In 1973, the couple gets divorced. Pierre-Alain teaches at Université du Québec à Chicoutimi and distance is straining the relationship. However, this doesn't last. In 1980, he's back in Montreal for good, working as a professor at ETS. He eventually becomes the first director of the Mechanical Engineering program and later, the dean of undergraduate studies.

Her father's career path influences Barbara's professional development. Her brother, Jean-Christophe, says that the connection between his father and his sister became stronger when she enrolled in pure sciences at Collège de Bois-de-Boulogne. After that, it's not surprising to see her pursue her studies at École Polytechnique, especially since she has another source of inspiration…. "My father was interested in engineering; my mother was interested in the advancement of the status of women," explains Jean-Christophe.

Being a woman in a traditionally male world doesn't even begin to intimidate a woman like Barbara!

A few months before the end of her studies at Polytechnique, she's already working with her father as an assistant to train students in his mechanical engineering lab at ETS. She makes some money, gains experience, and most of all, the certainty of having chosen the right career.

But Barbara has other interests. Music, for example. In primary school, her mother enrolled her and her brother at École du Sacré-Coeur in Sherbrooke, where the family was living. This public school offered serious musical training. Barbara learned to play piano and violin.

Barbara (right) during Christmas vacation in December 1979, in her father's second home in Berthierville. With her are her friend, Geneviève Marchand, and her brother, Jean-Christophe Daigneault.

Birthday dinner for Barbara (in red) and Jean-Christophe (front, left) with their friends, Marc Goulet and Geneviève Marchand, in Berthierville in March 1981.

When the trio moves to Montreal, the two children are enrolled at École Secondaire Joseph-François-Perrault, also known for its music program. Barbara trades her violin for a double bass, while Jean-Christophe dabbles with the cello.

But what he's really interested in is the developing choir. That's not the case for Barbara, who would prefer to be a soloist. She has even taken private singing lessons. So, she switches from a concentration in music to a music elective, which frees her schedule for science classes.

Barbara and Jean-Christophe get along well. Well enough to live together when, in the spring of 1989, their mother leaves Montreal to settle in the countryside. Barbara finds their new apartment on Ontario Street, next to one of her friends' place. Their father gives them three very simple rules: take care of yourself, study to get good grades, and live in harmony.

Everyone is doing their thing and it's all working nicely. Jean-Christophe has fun going out with his group of friends. Barbara, more quiet, dates Éric-Alexis, also an engineering student. She's twenty-two, she has found her professional path in mechanical engineering, and she's in love.

On December 6, 1989, she leaves the apartment with a vibrant "Bye" full of accusations. Her brother ate some of the kidneys that she cooked two days before. The door closes. Jean-Christophe will never see her again.

After December 6

Pierre-Alain, who passed away on October 15, 1996, always maintained that his heart stopped beating on December 6, 1989. But this heart that wasn't beating continued to take action for his daughter.

On December 6, at 5:45 p.m., Pierre-Alain calls his son: "Have you heard from Barbara?" "Uh, no...."

"I had been studying all day and I wasn't aware of what had happened," says Jean-Christophe today.

Half an hour later, he gets another call from his father who says he can't sit still and is leaving for Polytechnique. Hours later, he's one of the parents who have to identify their dead daughter. "At 2:00 in the morning, he came to tell me the news. I couldn't believe it. My parents were devastated."

In the following days, they face a new surprise: colleagues, students, even complete strangers spontaneously offer sometimes considerable sums of money to Pierre-Alain. What to do with these donations? Keeping the money is out of the question. He consults the family, who supports the idea of creating a fund in Barbara's memory.

The money is entrusted to ETS who, at the end of January 1990, creates the Fonds Barbara-Daigneault, which awards scholarships to female engineering students annually. Pierre-Alain himself will make significant contributions to the fund. As of today, nearly seventy students have benefited from this scholarship.

"My parents wanted to encourage women to go into this profession and get off the beaten path," says Jean-Christophe. "It wasn't so much about rewarding the best female student, but about rewarding those who have the best academic and social balance—to encourage young people to have a balanced life. My mother believed in this orientation."

There is another gesture of support from ETS students. A few days after the tragedy, they propose to charge a symbolic admission fee for the end-of-year party. They will sell white roses and give the proceeds to an organization still to be determined. They opt for the Fonds Barbara-Daigneault. This selling of roses takes place every year.

For the family members, preferring to be discreet, the fund was a way to compensate for their absence at the commemorations. They were worried about bringing attention to themselves by showing up at public events. "When a public presence was absolutely necessary, we were represented by Marie-Claire Gagnon [Pierre-Alain's partner], who did a lot for us and for my father," says Jean-Christophe.

However, there's one ceremony to which they choose to participate that brings Barbara back to École Polytechnique for good....

"Barbara's ashes were kept in a small box," recalls her brother. "The only person who would visit it was my father. He thought: Barbara's dream was to be at Polytechnique and get her diploma." So, Pierre-Alain has an idea. He consults Henriette, who agrees with him....

He then reaches out to Louis Courville, whom he knew as the interim president of Polytechnique in 1989. He asks: "My daughter was cremated. Polytechnique was her entire life. Could you keep the ashes?"

"You don't say no to a father who asks for that," says Courville. "But where could we keep them?"[21] He finally suggests that the ashes be embedded in one of the columns outside the cafeteria, which is currently being renovated—a discreet place, protected from vandalism, right next to the black granite commemorative plaque that will be affixed to the wall. The last step is to check with the person in charge of the work that this won't weaken the column.

Sometime later, the immediate family attends a 15-minute ceremony. The urn is slipped inside the column, which is immediately sealed.

Since then, a modest plaque of a few centimeters, bearing a short epitaph, marks the presence of the ashes:

21. Interview with Louis Courville, June 21, 2019 (my translation).

Anne-Marie Edward

SUNDAY, DECEMBER 3, 1989. The end of semester exams are coming up at Polytechnique. But Anne-Marie Edward doesn't have her nose in her books. She's in the Laurentides, at Mont Habitant, where she's participating in a skiathlon to raise money for cancer research.

Skiing is one of her passions. In the fall, she joined, and has since been training with, the Université de Montréal ski team. A great achievement for a woman who grew up encouraged to play outdoors. Thanks to that, she excels in several sports.

Preparing for exams and competing at the same time is not at all surprising for a woman like her, even though she's in her first year at Polytechnique, which is very demanding. "A force of nature," her relatives and her friends spontaneously say.

In fact, she's a Jack-of-all-trades who's not afraid of anything. And is used to doing everything at the same time.

For her family, the image is clear: Anne-Marie is the white water kayaking, survival camping in remote places, and rock-climbing woman. She's the one who takes Cristo—the white horse belonging to a neighbor in Shediac, New Brunswick, where the family owns a century-old house—out for rides.

Anne-Marie with Cristo, the horse belonging to a neighbor in New Brunswick.

She takes such good care of Cristo that it's as if it belongs to her. Her mother, Suzanne Laplante-Edward, used to say "It's impossible to make her clean her room, but cleaning the neighbor's stable on a Saturday afternoon, no problem!" recalls Jim Edward, nicknamed Jimmy, Anne-Marie's beloved brother.[22]

She insists on being at the helm of the family sailboat, a 14-foot vessel. She particularly likes stormy weather, with waves and strong winds. Her brother Jim remembers the day when she had fun capsizing the boat and righting it again "up to fifty-six times in a row!"[23]

Jimmy, her partner in crime…. The family legend has it that he "discovered" his little sister when she was born in 1968. After coming back from the hospital, while this young boy of almost two years was sleeping in his bed, his parents put their newborn down in her bedroom…. Awakened by cooing, Jimmy gets up, approaches the crib…then runs to the living room, yelling to his mother that he just found a baby! The anecdote stayed, and so did their unshakable bond.

22. Correspondence with Jim Edward, September 20, 2019 (my translation).
23. Interview with Jim Edward, June 14, 2019 (my translation).

Anne-Marie is tireless. And yet, she knows how to slow down. "She had a peaceful soul and radiated a profound serenity conducive to introspection," says Jim today.[24] She likes reading, she likes writing. She left behind three diaries and some letters.

Languages also interest her. Her father, James, a New Brunswick native, speaks English, while her mother, Suzanne, is a Francophone from Montreal. So, Anne-Marie is bilingual. To these two languages, she adds Spanish, which she learns in high school, at Collège Sainte-Marcelline, and can speak and write fluently.

Being trilingual is not that rare in Quebec at the time.... But she also learns German in preparation for a student exchange in Bavaria. In the end, she will be at it every Saturday morning...for three years.

When Anne-Marie arrives at John Abbott College, she's happy. She throws herself into a whirlwind of extracurricular activities! Her list is long: kayaking, mountaineering, adventure, riding, softball, soccer, and she even earns a lifeguard certificate.

Anne-Marie and her brother, Jim, during a road trip to Gaspésie in the summer of 1989.

24. Correspondence with Jim Edward, op. cit.

She still finds time to take care of disabled youth at the Stewart Hall Cultural Centre and the YMCA in Pointe-Claire. She plays piano and guitar and develops a talent for sewing. So, she designs and makes her first dress.

She spreads out her classes in order to accommodate everything. She'll take two-and-a-half years to finish her studies in pure and applied sciences. She obtains her diploma in December 1988.

Her father remains skeptical about her operating mode. He discreetly leaves the poem *Ambition*, by the great American author Edgar Albert Guest, on the desk in her bedroom. She learns a lesson from it, which she notes in her diary: "I have to think about doing better than just enough!"

When she starts at École Polytechnique in January, she has a clear goal: to make a career in chemical engineering, a specialty to which she was introduced during her summer jobs, in 1988 and then in 1989, at Monsanto Canada, where her father works.

At the end of the summer of 1989, she takes a road trip to Gaspésie with her brother and a few girlfriends, before going to the family house in New Brunswick. There, after a rather rainy week, rich in exchanges with her relatives, she leaves a note in the "guest book:"

> This place will always bring back the memory of wonderful days: the summer of my sixteen years, with my dear aunt Hélène, long hours scanning the beaches of Parlee Beach, attractive men, the sea... This week was also fun, but calm and relaxing in front of the fire. I loved it!

On October 25, she celebrates her 21st birthday. She's cherished, loved, supported. Life is beautiful. Life is waiting for her.

After December 6

At her funeral, this appetite for life is highlighted: "Anne-Marie saw life as a privilege. She gave her love to everyone and her friendship was unconditional. Dedicate your first exams to her.... And above all, don't worry about your grades since they were absolutely not important to her."

A friend says about her: "It would be easier to describe a gust of wind than to define Anne-Marie.... But those who were willing to get swept along in her wake had the chance to experience a strong and sincere friendship."

Anne-Marie left such a strong impression everywhere she went that her memory was honored soon after the tragedy.

In mid-December 1989, less than two weeks after the massacre, the employees of Monsanto Canada create the Fonds de bourse à la mémoire d'Anne-Marie Edward, pledging to match the donations made by the public.

Initially destined for the students of Polytechnique, in 1992 the scholarship is entrusted to the John Abbott College Foundation. It's still used to reward a student who, like Anne-Marie, distinguished himself or herself on an academic and social level. The selection committee takes into consideration students' social, academic, and community engagement, as well as their life balance.

In 2005, the Montreal borough of Pierrefonds-Roxboro decides to mark the tragic death of the young woman by creating a monument that will pay tribute to three female borough residents who were assassinated. The site "Dire Non à la violence" ("Say No to Violence") is laid out in Parc Grier. In addition to the murder of Anne-Marie, it marks the murders of Janet Kuchinsky, killed on one of the borough's bike paths, and Kelly-Ann Drummond, an elite athlete killed by her spouse. Three victims of violence against women, three powerful symbols that shouldn't be forgotten.

In April 2013, John Abbott College must name its science pavilion, inaugurated a few months earlier. The committee in charge of finding a name opts for Anne-Marie Edward Science Building. The recognition of the role of women in this sector is now clearly spelled out. Another way to never forget.

Finally, Anne-Marie's family is extremely involved after the tragedy. Family members participate in the creation of the Fondation des victimes du 6 décembre contre la violence, of which Suzanne is the first president, holding that position for several years, organizing the commemorations from 1991 to 1999. Also, from 1991 until 2001, she traveled to Canadian universities, from Halifax to Vancouver, with the support of Air Canada, speaking about the lives of the fourteen victims of the massacre.

The Edward family also contribute to the effort to obtain a gun registry, Jim being one of the spokespersons for the Coalition for Gun Control. The family has also been a constant presence at the commemorations organized over the last thirty years.

Maud Haviernick

IN DECEMBER 1989, Maud Haviernick is twenty-nine. These few extra years set her apart from her colleagues who, like her, are doing their undergraduate degree at Polytechnique. She didn't take the traditional path, "science studies in cégep, then enrollment at Polytechnique." She got there very differently.

Since forever, Maud has been an artist. She particularly likes sculpting. She has good taste, originality, and is never short on ideas.

After high school, she naturally opts for the program in Interior Design at Cégep du Vieux Montréal. She develops an interest in designing spaces for individual and communal life. What follows is logical: she enrolls in the undergraduate Environmental Design program at UQAM.

It's a transitional period for Maud. She meets her future spouse, Serges Gagnon, her great love until her death. Settled in Laval, in the neighborhood of Sainte-Rose, the couple sets up a dedicated space in their house for the young woman's creative projects.

As for her studies, they confirm that she's on the right track. She rapidly realizes projects such as the design of the student café in the Design Department. It's thrilling...but she wants to go further.

After a stint on the job market, Maud realizes that her diploma, obtained in 1984, doesn't allow her to rise above the position of project manager. As talented a designer as she may be, as important her responsibilities, final decisions will always be out of her reach because, on a construction site, they belong to engineers. But this young, natural-born leader wants to have the upper hand and the last word.

"If I want to be the one who decides, I have no choice. I have to get this diploma!" she tells her relatives when talking about her new goal to study at Polytechnique.[25]

Her large family—one brother and three sisters—is surprised by Maud's new scientific orientation, but everyone is convinced that she'll succeed in conquering the obstacles that hinder her professional growth.

However, this requires a great dose of humility. She has to go back to cégep to take science classes, something which, up until this day, she had shown no interest in whatsoever…. Never mind. No time for dithering: she starts at Collège Lionel-Groulx.

She has to work hard. Her sister, Martine, who is studying to become a biologist, helps her find her way in this new scientific world where she's not entirely comfortable yet.

Maud and Serges Gagnon, her spouse and great love.

25. Interview with Martine Haviernick, June 5, 2019.

Maud in front of UQAM's main pavilion in September 1982 during her undergraduate studies in Environmental Design.

But the Haviernick children are resourceful. Sylvie, the oldest, has paved the way. She's the first one in the family to have gone to university, and she encourages her brother and sisters to surpass themselves, despite their modest origins. Her mantra is: "If you want to go that far, well, do it!"

The lesson bears fruit because Rodolphe Haviernick and Réjeanne Moore's children all graduate from university, even if it takes a lot of effort. To make ends meet, Maud works as a waitress in some of Montreal's best restaurants and, later, at the restaurant Les Menus Plaisirs in Sainte-Rose.

Studying at Polytechnique requires a lot of energy. During exam periods, when she's unable to concentrate, Maud goes to her mother's in Deux-Montagnes. Réjeanne is more than happy to see her daughter work at the kitchen table. She takes care of her, the stress goes down, and everything goes well.

As a specialization, Maud chose materials engineering. In the fall semester of 1989, she's in her third year. Once again, the prospect of the end-of-semester exams increases her anxiety. But when December 6 arrives, Maud is ready to present her project in professor Jean-Paul Baïlon's class.

After December 6

Martine is at work when she hears on the radio that a gunman is shooting people at Polytechnique.

She joins her mother and her brother at her parents' house in Deux-Montagnes, where all three live. They call back and forth with Nadine and Sylvie, Maud's two other sisters. "The more time went by without any news, the less hope we had. Yet, I spent hours and hours imagining that Maud was hiding somewhere in the school, terrified, and that she was waiting to come out...," remembers Martine.

Around 11:30 p.m., Sylvie goes to the university accompanied by a work colleague. At 3:30 a.m., they receive the confirmation that Maud is one of the victims. A little later, police officers from Deux-Montagnes announce the sad news to her mother…. It's over. Maud won't get to the end of her journey. But maybe others will….

In 1992, UQAM creates the Fonds capitalisé Maud-Haviernick. The funds raised make it possible to give, every two years, an excellence award in her name. But starting in 2019, thanks to the efforts of her close friend Maurice Cloutier, the award is every year. It rewards a recently minted female undergraduate student in Environmental Design, who is pursuing a graduate degree.

In addition, in 2000, the parish Saint-Agapit in Deux-Montagnes creates the Fonds en mémoire de Maud Haviernick to fight violence against women. The management of the fund is taken over in 2003 by the new parish Sainte-Marie-du-Lac. Thanks to this fund, the parish can financially support organizations that help women. It also makes possible the installation of a monument dedicated to victims of femicide.

The Haviernicks are among the families who, in the wake of the tragedy, set up the Fondation des victimes du 6 décembre contre la violence. They will be deeply involved in the foundation, as well as in the group PolySeSouvient, created in 2009.

Barbara-Maria Klucznik-Widajewicz

BARBARA-MARIA KLUCZNIK-WIDAJEWICZ is a student in December 1989, but not at École Polytechnique. She goes to the Faculty of Nursing at Université de Montréal.

In fact, she's already an engineer. Born in Poland in October 1958, she obtains her Master's degree in Engineering in 1983 from the Wroclaw University of Economics and Business, located in Wroclaw, her hometown. She studies education for another two years, which makes it possible for her to get hired at a primary school in the city. She loves the field of education and working with kids, who love her in return.

Furthermore, since she was sixteen, she's been seeing a young man her age, a future student in medicine named Witold Widajewicz.

Witold is very taken with this young woman, nicknamed Basia by her family. She's brilliant and has so many interests: she likes jazz, she paints, she wants to learn everything. As soon as they meet, they become insepara-ble. They're still in school when they decide to get married in September 1981.

A few months later, on December 13, 1981, martial law is declared in the country in an effort to crush the dissent led by the movement Solidarność

against the Communist regime, in power in Poland as well as in every country in Eastern Europe and in the Soviet Union. This is years before the fall of the Berlin Wall and the end of the Cold War.

Like millions of Poles, Barbara-Maria and Witold join Solidarność. They're very active, secretly printing tracts and distributing them. The government's iron grip on the country convinces them to plan an escape. There's no future for them in a Poland that is closing itself to the outside world.

They want to go to Montreal, which Witold, nicknamed Witek, visited during the 1976 Summer Olympics—a gift from an aunt and uncle who have been living there for a long time. He brought back fond memories, surprised to be so comfortable in a place where he found a sense of community and a defense of local culture similar to what he was experiencing at home, as he still says today.[26]

Barbara-Maria and her husband Witold in their apartment in Park-Extension, Montreal, in 1988.

The couple wants to leave, but Poland is not inclined to issue passports to its doctors and scientists. While they wait, they discreetly prepare their move to Montreal. Barbara-Maria, who already speaks Polish, Russian, English, and German, takes French classes at Alliance Française.

An opportunity finally presents itself in July 1986. They manage to cross the border and reach Germany. Witold's aunt, now a widow, has agreed to sponsor them so they can come to Montreal. They arrive on April 23, 1987. "It was an adventure, our great escape!" says Witold.

The young couple doesn't want to depend on anyone. Two days after their arrival, Witold finds a night job in a retirement home. Barbara babysits the children of a family in Mount-Royal, reconnecting with the childhood world she had gotten to know as a teacher in Wroclaw.

Witold wants to practice medicine in Quebec, so he goes back to school. However, he comes to understand that the positions available to young doctors are in the regions, where it's less likely that Barbara-Maria can work as an engineer. Yet, it's out of the question that the couple be separated.

Barbara-Maria during a weekend escape with her husband in 1988.

Isn't there work for a nurse anywhere in Quebec? And she likes helping people anyway.

26. Interview with Witold Widajewicz, June 27, 2019.

She takes a few remedial classes in Cégep and in September 1989, just a month shy of her thirty-first birthday, she's officially enrolled in the undergraduate program in Nursing. The only Pole taking the entry exams, she does so well that in her first semester, she's awarded an excellence grant normally reserved for female students in their second year. The dean at the time said of Barbara-Maria that she was "the pride of the faculty."

And she's friendly so everywhere she goes, she makes friends. The thirty-something couple enjoy attending student parties and love Montreal life. "We were poor, but we were happy," says Witold. The couple remain politically engaged and closely follow the events in Eastern Europe, which culminate with the fall of the Berlin Wall in November 1989—a major turning point in the history of the 20th century.

Their new life still comes with sacrifices: for example, not being able to go back to Poland, even for a short visit. Pawel, Barbara-Maria's brother, eight years her junior and very attached to her, got married the same year Basia and Witek arrived in Montreal.

In 1988, the newlyweds have a daughter, Sara, and they make Barbara-Maria her godmother. From then on, many letters and photos are exchanged, and many gifts travel from the aunt to the child: "the most beautiful things she could buy in Montreal,"[27] says Pawel.

Barbara-Maria and Witold are so busy with their studies that they often eat their meals on the Université de Montréal campus. And of all the cafeterias available, the one they adopted is in École Polytechnique.

That's where they meet on this late afternoon of December 6, 1989. Barbara-Maria has just paid for her dinner while her husband, not far behind her, is still filling his tray. She makes her way to a quiet table, near a column. Suddenly, there are loud noises and confusion. With no time to see anything, Witold is dragged by the crowd towards the kitchen. There's been a hold-up, people around him are saying.

When he's evacuated through the emergency exit, he doesn't know what happened to his wife.

27. Correspondence with Pawel Klucznik, July 24, 2019 (my translation).

Barbara-Maria, her brother Pawel, and her mother Anna on a trip outside the city in the summer of 1976.

After December 6

Witold Widajewicz feels very alone during the two days the body of his beloved Barbara-Maria is on view in the Hall of Honour of Université de Montréal. Very alone also during the funeral at the Notre-Dame Basilica. Family and friends are far away in Poland—not by his side.

He feels all the more alone since his wife died in a country where the couple came in search of freedom, and in this year 1989, their native country finally frees itself from the Communist grip they had both fled. What a bitter irony.

Witold doesn't even have the money to send the body back to Poland. He turns to Polytechnique, which agrees to cover the transportation costs.

Barbara-Maria is buried on December 15, 1989 in the Catholic cemetery of Wroclaw, after a funeral that brings many people together. Witold then goes back to Montreal to finish his studies.

But the weight of the loss is so great that he ends up leaving Quebec, first for Manitoba, then for British Columbia, where he still lives today. He now works in legal psychiatry—which is not a coincidence, he says.

In 1994, Polytechnique brings Barbara-Maria's parents from Poland so they can participate in the commemoration ceremonies on the 5th anniversary of the tragedy.

And in 1990, the Faculty of Nursing awards a scholarship in the name of Barbara-Maria Klucznik to a second-year undergraduate female student with an excellent academic record who needs financial support. This scholarship, in the amount of $5,000, is still awarded annually.

Maryse Laganière

MARYSE LAGANIÈRE goes to École Polytechnique but not as a student. She's an employee, working as a secretary in Financial Services. However, she's not much older than the students who attend the school.

Born in April 1964 in Grondines, she's the thirteenth and last child of Aline Tessier and Égide Laganière. She's two years old when her family leaves the region of Mauricie to move to the Hochelaga-Maisonneuve neighborhood of Montreal.

After studying computer science at Cégep de Maisonneuve, in her early twenties Maryse gets a position at Polytechnique, first in the Scientific Research Services, then in finances. Like the young women who study there, Polytechnique is the place where her life is going to take a turn. In her case, it's because she meets her great love, Jean-François Larivée—Jeff, as everyone calls him.

Their story begins in early 1986. Jeff has spent the holidays in Florida with his family. But his stay takes a worrisome turn when a hurricane forces him to delay his return. He's an engineering student at Polytechnique, and he's afraid that he'll get back too late to pay his tuition for the next semester.

On Monday, January 6, he rushes to the school's Financial Services, aware that he missed the deadline for his payment. But he has the money and reasons to justify his tardiness.

Maryse listens to him. He's so taken by her "magnificent blue eyes"[28] that he gets mixed up in the details. She interrupts him to go plead his case with the person in charge. He notices that she blushed when she answered him.

So, he starts hanging around her, wooing her discreetly, which suits this shy young woman. They see each other more and more, in the school or outside, to enjoy Mount Royal, where Polytechnique is located.

She tells him about her large family, whom she is close to. In particular, she's very affected by the death of her brother-in-law, husband of her sister Yolande, who lives in Acton Vale. Jeff appreciates her great sensitivity.

In early November 1986, he finally works up the courage to invite her to see a movie...and to take her hand. The movie over, she follows him home, to his parents' house in Laval. They find refuge in the basement, with the parents upstairs.

Jeff and Maryse on an expedition during their honeymoon in Punta Cana in August 1989.

The rest is pure romance, like a moment suspended in time: "We sit down, perfectly still, in front of a television that we don't turn on," recounts Jean-François. "At the end of this very beautiful moment, I look at her and I say: 'Do you want to be my girlfriend?' Her eyes filled with joy, she says: 'Yes.' I push a little more: 'How about you? Are you going to ask me?' She says: 'Do you want to be my boyfriend?' I say: 'Yes.'" And that's it, they were set for life.

In the spring of 1987, the couple decide to live together. Nothing more logical, and nothing revolutionary when we look at the situation decades later. But in Quebec at the time, not all families accepted that couples live together before marriage. Attitudes were changing but not as fast as we would believe.

So, it's unbeknownst to Maryse's parents that they rent and furnish an apartment in the neighborhood of Rosemont in Montreal. Maryse has just turned twenty-three. On July 1, Jeff moves in by himself. Only fourteen

Maryse on her parents' balcony before her marriage to Jeff.

28. Correspondence with Jean-François Larivée, September 8, 2019.

days later does the couple finally muster the courage to tell Maryse's parents that she's moving out. But they're very firm. Despite any opinions, convictions, and objections the Laganières may have, they're moving into "their" apartment. They're determined and they're happy.

Two years later, the couple is able to buy a small building on Bourbonnière Avenue, south of Ontario Street, in Hochelaga-Maisonneuve, the neighborhood where the Laganières live. Resistance has melted; Maryse's family respects the couple's decisions, recognizing that they are serious in building their future.

During that same summer, another step is taken: on August 12, 1989, Jeff and Maryse get married. The ceremony is followed by a honeymoon on the beaches of Punta Cana. Their happiness is written all over their faces.

"She had a very unique way of sharing her feelings. Her face would simply glow from the emotion she was feeling," says her husband. "She had an extraordinary smile," confirms Guy Brunelle, a colleague of the young woman at Polytechnique, who was very fond of her.[29]

"We could understand each other with one look," says Jean-François. "When we went out, I could read in her eyes if she was comfortable or if we had to leave. This complicity filled us with joy."

They find happiness in day-to-day life. Maryse, for example, likes needlework such as knitting and embroidery. She decorates their apartment with her creations. Nothing extravagant. Nothing that might make people talk. A quiet couple living a beautiful story. Also a couple who wanted a child.

"When she died, I looked at her calendar. She was five days 'late,'" says Jean-François. She was pregnant; he's always been convinced of it.

29. Interview with Guy Brunelle, June 19, 2019.

After December 6

Over the last thirty years, Jean-François has given several interviews and participated in many news stories dedicated to the Polytechnique massacre. And he has attended the commemorations. He also supported the creation of the Fondation des victimes du 6 décembre contre la violence and got involved with PolySeSouvient.

He has never hesitated to talk about his profound distress, about the devastation he felt. He still says it today: "I lost my best friend, my confidante, the person I wanted to spend my life with."

The young woman's funeral doesn't take place during the ceremony at the Notre-Dame Basilica on Monday, December 11, 1989. The family wants to mourn in a more personal and intimate setting.

The funeral mass is held the next day, on Tuesday, December 12, at Église Saint-Clément in Hochelaga-Maisonneuve, after a wake at the funeral home next door. But the concept of an intimate ceremony has to be rethought. Nearly a thousand people show up at the funeral home to pay homage to Maryse. And there are as many more people inside the church and out the front door during the religious ceremony. Five buses have been made available to Polytechnique students so they could go.

Throughout the celebration, fourteen candles shine on the altar as a reminder of the collective tragedy. In his eulogy, Abbot Paul Delâge points out the sad paradox of death coming so soon after a wedding—a wedding he officiated only four months earlier. To the day.

Maryse Leclair

MARYSE DOES WHATEVER she wants. A bit rebellious, she's determined not to adhere to classic ideas of femininity. As a teenager, she wants to be an astronaut. That says it all!

As a child, she's so good in her role of eldest that it sometimes looks like authoritarianism towards her three sisters. However, when it comes to her—and this is a wonderful contradiction—she absolutely resists authority. Is it surprising when you're the daughter of a police officer?

But her father, Pierre Leclair, can also be a good guide to follow. He was a Scout Leader, so his four daughters joined the Girl Guides program and moved through the levels, from *Brownies* to *Rangers*. Maryse enjoys Guiding. At fifteen, the required age, she moved to the *Rangers* level. At this level, you can lead your own adventures, there are more challenges, and the humanitarian approach is more developed.

Maryse already has a strong personality. Case in point, she only spends one year at Collège Regina Assumpta in Montreal, where her parents have enrolled her for high school. The uniform and strict discipline don't work for her. So much so that she convinces her parents to transfer her to a different school.

She ends up at Polyvalente Mont-de-La Salle in Laval. She likes the atmosphere of this progressive school where there's no uniform. She makes friends, with whom she shares a common passion, typical of the 1980s: the British punk movement and the Montreal New Wave scene. Music, clothes, hairstyle, nonchalance, the small group adopts it all! Indeed, when she can't find the right outfits, Maryse makes her own, tailoring and sewing clothes that she likes—including the dress for her graduation ball.

Admittedly, the teenager is turbulent, but you have to have fun in life. Living in suburban Laval with a police officer as a father wasn't very cool, says Pierre with tenderness.[30] But even then, he wasn't too worried, certain that it would pass.

And with time, Maryse changes, evolves, settles down. She also shows remarkable aptitude for sports that require strength and flexibility: handball, skiing, rock climbing, windsurfing.... She comes up with the idea of spending a summer at the Canadian military training camp in Valcartier. People around her are skeptical, but when Maryse wants something....

The training is supposed to last two months, but it's demanding and Maryse injures her knee. She decides to leave before the end, recognizing that it's too hard. "Too rigid for her," summarizes Pierre, ten years after the massacre.[31]

When it comes time to go to university, she chooses École des Hautes Études Commerciales. But she's disappointed—it doesn't provide the creative professional environment that she needs. She changes her orientation and enrolls at Polytechnique in Materials Engineering.

She also has responsibilities. Mom and Dad pay their daughters' tuition, but they have to help. Maryse lives in Montreal, where she shares an apartment with Agathe Simard, another student from Polytechnique, and she has to pay her part of the rent.

She has several student jobs and is particularly thrilled with her experience working for Produits d'Emballage Ball Canada at Baie-d'Urfé in the summer of 1988. She is the only woman among eighty workers. She feels heard, respected, and appreciated.

30. Interview with Pierre Leclair, May 22, 2019.
31. Isabelle Hachey, "La lumière au bout du tunnel" [The light at the end of the tunnel], *La Presse*, November 27, 1999.

Finally, she has someone in her life, a student from Polytechnique named Benoît—a discreet man who nonetheless wants to express his affection for this love from the past.[32]

In December 1989, they've been together for several months already—an important relationship for the young woman who's turning twenty-four on the next January 3. She and Benoît are often together, studying, traveling, dreaming up new projects. Maryse is always willing! "If I had told her that it would be fun to go to Nepal, within the next minute she would have booked the flights and gone to the airport to wait for me! She was very inspiring; she was a natural-born winner," he remembers.

With a hint of craziness! "You should have seen her car! An old Honda Civic covered in graffiti. She went to a party and someone came up with the idea to paint her car. She agreed and the result was...mind-boggling! One time, she gave a ride to my mother, who was a little shy to drive around in such a weird-looking car. To ease her concerns, Maryse told her that when you're in the car, you can't see what it looks like. That was so typically Maryse! She was living her life the way she wanted to and wasn't at all bothered by what other people thought."

Maryse, clearly happy with her Christmas present in 1987, next to her sister Sophie.

On Sunday, December 3, the couple go to her parents' house in Laval. Maryse is radiant. She's wearing a beautiful red sweater that she bought for the holidays. She was impatient to try it on and is planning on wearing it again the next Wednesday for the presentation of her group project at Polytechnique.

On December 6, Benoît has planned to attend her presentation but he's late and the class had to move to a different classroom. By the time it would take him to get there, Maryse's presentation will be over. "So, I went to the student lounge to wait for her. Then some students came running in and told us that there was a shooter in the school."

At the cottage in Magog, Maryse surrounded by her sisters Madeleine (left) and Geneviève (right).

32. Correspondence with Benoît, September 10, 2019.

Because They Were Women

After December 6

Maryse's death deeply captures the attention of the public. She's Lépine's last victim, the one who was presenting when he entered the classroom, the one who said "help me" after being hit by a bullet, the one he stabbed to death before committing suicide. And she's the one who is found by her father because of his job. She will be the first deceased woman whose name is made public.

That night, Pierre, in charge of communications at SPCUM, goes inside Polytechnique to evaluate the situation, and be able to answer the journalists who rushed towards him as soon as he arrived. While making his way through the school, he gets to a classroom on the third floor where the lights are on. He sees his daughter lying on the stage next to Lépine's body....

A police officer is already guarding the crime scene, with strict orders not to let anyone in, including a father. Pierre must turn around and leave.

That's how, pale and broken, he bumps into his friend and colleague Jacques Duchesneau, who is participating in the investigation. Duchesneau sends him home. Journalists and television viewers, who had heard him say that he would be back with some news, won't see him again....

At home, when Louise sees him back so soon, she understands everything. With her daughter Sophie, they throw themselves into his arms. Geneviève and Madeleine, their two other daughters who live in Montreal, join them a few minutes later. "Then a dozen people came to comfort us," remembers Pierre. The Mayor of Laval Gilles Vaillancourt also visits them, as he visits the families of Maud Haviernick and Hélène Colgan, who live in the same city.

Over the following weeks, the Leclairs receive over four hundred messages of condolence from Quebec, Canada, US, Europe, UK, and even Australia. Over the holidays, their next-door neighbors turned off their Christmas lights as a sign of respect for their loss.

The trauma is great for the family. Pierre had already planned to leave SPCUM for the Service de police de Sainte-Foy, where he eventually becomes Chief. Moving to a different city proves very healing.

Then, optimism and a deep love of life take over. From the first anniversary of the tragedy, the resilience of the Leclairs is striking. Pierre and Louise, Maryse's mother (both of them now deceased), talk about the solidarity they were shown and the important lesson they learned that continues to guide them: "People are not that mean."[33]

Since then, every year members of the family attend the commemorations of the massacre.

As for Benoît, he says: "I was very shaken by what happened at Polytechnique. I didn't feel the same as the rest of the population, which was horrified by the tragedy. For me, I lost the one I loved. Eventually it faded, but it never goes away. Every year, I take the day off on December 6 and I visit her grave. And for the last few years, I've been going to the ceremony on Mount Royal."

"I have two daughters, who are adults now. I've tried to instill in them values of autonomy, independence, and kindness. I remind them regularly to not worry about what other people think, as Maryse was so good at doing. I like to tell them often that we can't change how other people think; we can only change how we think."

33. André Pépin, "Le monde n'est pas si méchant" ["People are not that mean"], *La Presse*, December 1, 1990.

Anne-Marie Lemay

ANNE-MARIE LEMAY is thinking about medicine when she decides to become an engineer. It might seem like an unusual connection, but it isn't at all. The young woman knows it first-hand.

When she was a teenager, a friend her age lost the use of his legs. For two years, accompanied by a girlfriend, she visits him on a weekly basis to help him go through the movements that will help re-establish the connection between his brain and his limbs. This re-adaptation process, supervised by a doctor, lasts until the friend is transferred to a specialized institution.

From this experience, Anne-Marie learns how important mechanical devices and prostheses are in compensating for disabilities. But while doctors provide care, engineers are the ones who design this equipment. So, two careers are possible for someone like her, who wishes to take care of others.

That's a character trait she's had since she was very young. As a child, she freely expresses her affection for people, even those she barely knows. Michelle Proulx and Pierre Lemay, her parents, remember a little girl who is responsible, easy-going, and doesn't argue over useless details.[34]

34. Interview with Michelle Proulx and Pierre Lemay, June 7, 2019.

She stays the same as she grows older. She doesn't dwell on problems and avoids conflicts. Her outgoing personality is attractive—people like being around her.

A resident of Boucherville, where she was born in June 1967, Anne-Marie attends Collège Charles-Lemoyne, a high school with campuses in Longueuil and Sainte-Catherine. For cégep, she crosses the river to study at Collège de Maisonneuve in Montreal.

When it comes time to choose a university program, she deems her grades too low to go into medicine. Instead, she applies to engineering programs at three universities: McGill, Sherbrooke, and Polytechnique. The latter opens its doors to her.

Anne-Marie immediately enjoys the school. A sociable person, working as part of a team—because an engineer never works alone—perfectly suits her. It creates strong groups and reduces competitiveness in a demanding field that many will have to abandon at the end of their first year, short of getting the grades to keep going. Since the students have to create work together, they also have to learn to move towards a common goal without getting in conflict with each other.

New Year's Eve 1989. Anne-Marie (second from the left), her parents, and her friends from the choir in Boucherville.

Anne-Marie finishes her first year and can now choose a specialty. Faithful to her teenage preoccupations, she opts for mechanical engineering.

She moves to Montreal, renting an apartment on Wilderton Avenue, not far from Université de Montréal. She shares it with two girlfriends who, like her, come from Boucherville. The three friends go home on the weekends for an activity they all have in common: singing.

Indeed, singing is Anne-Marie's other passion. She takes her first piano lessons at eight and, at the same time, is initiated to the pleasures of singing through sol-fa. She soon joins the children's choir of the parish Saint-Sébastien in Boucherville, which performs on Sundays at "children's mass."

As they grow into teenagers, several members of the young choir switch over to another choir created by a boy their age. Anne-Marie is among them. The choir still sings at church, now at regular mass, but it also performs on other stages.

Isabel, Anne-Marie's sister, Pierre, their father, and Anne-Marie at a wedding.

For the young woman, this form of expression is vital. This is not surprising since her father also sings. Pierre, introduced to singing as a child, is a member of an operetta troupe—the Théâtre Lyrique de Boucherville—which, in 1997, becomes the Théâtre Lyrique de la Montérégie.

Cheerful but determined, Anne-Marie doesn't let prejudices stop her. In 1989, looking for a summer job, she decides to apply to a local branch of Speedy Muffler, which specializes in car mechanics, in Saint-Hubert. She's hired to work at the front desk. Small detail: she's the first woman to work there!

In September 1989, an internship at Cascades Technologies confirms that she's on the right path. She works on drawing three-dimensional plans on the computer, which are then cut by a machine tool. She loves the experience.

Her organizational skills and her leadership also manifest themselves at school. She offers to coordinate the appointments of graduating students who must have their official graduation photo taken, at the end of their studies. It's a vast operation, more complex than it may seem. Not only is Anne-Marie in charge of the planning, she's also there during the photo sessions to fix a strand of hair, smooth out a crease, or ask for a smile....

And she's in love. His name is Laurent and he too, is an engineering student. He's among the men that Marc Lépine kicks out of the classroom before attacking the women. In the yearbook of this terrible school year of 1989–1990, Laurent writes: "I learned a lot at Polytechnique, but I also lost a lot."

After December 6

With a woman as sensitive as Anne-Marie, we have to talk about before December 6 in order to talk about her death. Because three times in her short life, she talked about it herself.

When she was five, she asked her father point-blank: "Dad, who's going to kill me?" She was too young to explain where this strange idea was coming from....

Years later, as she's learning to capsize a small sailboat and right it again, she gets caught in the ropes and is underwater for a little too long. But she comes out of the experience serene. This brush with death had seemed sweet to her.

Finally, there's the note she wrote at the end of a night of studying, on the eve of December 6: "Tomorrow is the last day of class...and the last day of my life. Wow, that sounds really depressing at 3:00 in the morning."

Hours later, her mother, Michelle, is listening to Michel Désautels's late afternoon show on Radio-Canada radio, when she suddenly hears the traffic commentator Roger Laroche wonder about the presence of several ambulances at Polytechnique. He talks about a shooter.

Michelle is uneasy; she feels like she's seeing Anne-Marie walk towards her. Immediately, she "knows." Her daughter is among the victims.

Laurent calls the Lemay's residence: "Is Anne-Marie there?" He's looking for her and hasn't found her yet. She's not in her apartment, or in the hospitals he contacted. Anne-Marie's parents rush to the university. At 2:00 a.m., they finally find out what happened to their daughter.

When it comes time to organize the funeral, the family opts for a ceremony in its parish. They don't attend the mortuary chapel at Université de Montréal. "We wanted to do things our own way," they say. Bring Anne-Marie back home, where they can pay personal tribute to her.

"Anne-Marie's choir and her father's operetta troupe asked to sing at her funeral, and everything fell into place," says Michelle. *Hymn of Jean Racine*, a piece by Gabriel Fauré that Anne-Marie particularly liked, is among the works interpreted by the emotional choir, which is missing a voice.

Some 700 people attend the ceremony presided by Bishop Bernard Hubert from the diocese of Saint-Jean-Longueuil. He says: "Everyone here must wonder where God was that day. Wonder no longer. It was a human act that caused this tragedy."

In March 1991, Boucherville gives Anne-Marie's name to the park behind École Secondaire De Mortagne, which has a running track as well as a soccer and a baseball field. Anne-Marie's parents, her sister, Isabel, and her boyfriend, Laurent, write a thank-you letter to the city. It says: "Maybe some youth, while playing in the park, will reflect on the fact that its name used to belong to a young person who, until recently, was laughing and running, full of life and energy."

Like other families of the young women who were assassinated, the Lemays will participate in the creation of the Fondation des victimes du 6 décembre contre la violence.

Sonia Pelletier

SONIA PELLETIER came to Montreal from a long way away, a small village in Gaspésie named Saint-Ulric, whose original name in the 19th century was Rivière-Blanche, like the river nearby that flows into the Saint Lawrence. A magnificent place, fifteen kilometers away from Matane.

Sonia was born there in 1961, the youngest of a large family that already includes five sisters and two brothers. She's a quiet child, cheerful, self-sufficient. And as soon as she starts school, she's the top of her class—she's awarded scholarships and wins all the contests.

The more she progresses in her studies, the more she becomes the pride of her family and the people around her. Her energy, her keen intellect, her memorable talent...these are the things people still remember today.

"She was a rather exceptional person," says her friend Sylvie Harrison. "A memorable person, the kind of person you don't meet very often in your life."[35]

She gets to know Sonia at Cégep de Rimouski. Sonia already has a DEC in Architectural Technology and is taking additional classes so she can enroll at École Polytechnique. The two students meet in a math class.

35. Interview with Sylvie Harrison, July 16, 2019 (my translation).

Sonia receiving
a scholarship.

– ※ –

Sonia liked sketching, and not only for class, remembers Sylvie. In Rimouski, she had a notebook in which she would draw people around her in charcoal. She also liked sewing, and had had her own sewing machine for a long time.

Given the workload, once she starts at Polytechnique, Sonia abandons sewing and drawing to fully concentrate on her studies. She continues to shine, receiving an excellence award given by Polytechnique.

In Montreal, the two friends live together, with Dannie, Sylvie's sister (who, in a curious turn of events, now lives in Saint-Ulric), as the third roommate.

The cohabitation, which will last three years, has its advantages. Sonia is a very good cook and she teaches Sylvie how to make homemade pasta. Cooking is a way for her to relax. "She would make very elaborate dishes and spend a lot of time at it," says Sylvie.[36] But her roommates had better like Gerry Boulet. Sonia loves his song *Toujours vivant* and plays it all the time in the apartment.

36. Correspondence with Sylvie Harrison, September 10, 2019 (my translation).

For Sonia, classes at Polytechnique ended on December 5, 1989. Those were the last classes of her last semester of her last year of undergraduate studies in mechanical engineering. Only exams are left, but she has nothing to worry about, "her last transcript [was] filled with As."[37] Plus, she already has a job. Getting her diploma is a formality.

But, since she's a generous person, and her classmates attended the presentation of her project in the previous class, she's determined to be there for them.

"Just before she left for class, I said to her: 'Let's go out afterwards!' But she really wanted to go, out of respect for people." No other choice, Sylvie has to wait to celebrate the end of the semester.

On December 6, Sonia sits at a desk in classroom C-230.4, where the last presentations of the mechanical engineering class are taking place. Nine women are present among dozens of men, and she's the oldest. She's twenty-eight.

After December 6

When journalists approach the family to get their first reaction after Sonia's death, the parents are too shaken to say anything. Her sister, Monique, steps in. Her words burst out like a cry from the heart: "She was our baby. She was resourceful, organized. You should have seen her go. We're devastated."[38]

The family is so far away that Sylvie is delegated to go to the university and handle the initial arrangements.

The young woman's body is then repatriated to Saint-Ulric. Her family doesn't attend the ceremony at the Notre-Dame Basilica—they deal with their pain discreetly, in private, without fuss.

Sonia's father, in particular, doesn't talk about it much. "But one time, he told me that every night, after saying his prayers, he would talk to Sonia,"

---

37. Interview by Nathalie Collard, Katia Gagnon, and Judith Lachapelle, "En souvenir d'elles" [In their memory], *La Presse*, December 6, 2014 (my translation).

38. Marie-Claude Lortie, "C'était notre bébé" ["She was our baby"], *La Presse*, December 8, 1989 (my translation).

confides Micheline, one of Sonia's sisters, to *La Presse* in 2014. Her father died four years after the tragedy.[39]

In 2009, after the film *Polytechnique* by Denis Villeneuve came out, her mother, Louise Poitras-Pelletier, then ninety years old, said that she had finally forgiven Marc Lépine. "Oh, it took a long time. And I forgave him for his mother," she confided to Radio-Canada.[40]

In July 2019, on the occasion of the celebration of its 150th anniversary and to mark the 30th anniversary of the tragedy, the municipality of Saint-Ulric renames a park near the river in honor of Sonia. The messages of support that flood Facebook when this is announced show how much Sonia, who had one day left for the big city, had never been forgotten.

39. Op. cit.

40. Jean-François Deschesnes, "La mère d'une victime réagit" [The mother of a victim speaks out], ici.radio-canada.ca, February 4, 2009.

Michèle Richard

IN LAC-MÉGANTIC where she comes from, who, among Michèle Richard's peers, doesn't know her? And no one is thinking about the Quebec star singer of the same name from that time. Their star, "their" Michèle, is the one from Polyvalente Montignac. Thirty years later, friends continue to share stories about her.

Lac-Mégantic is quite far from École Polytechnique and from Montreal, but already there are hints of the determined Michèle who will later carve a place for herself in the big city. At fourteen she's one of the founders, along with a tight-knit group of friends, of Maison des Jeunes de Mégantic, says her close friend Jean-Marc Dupont.[41]

It's a big endeavor. They have to convince the mayor, find a space, set it up, and obtain financing from Centraide Estrie. The young people are so invested in the project that the adults guiding them stay in the background.

"Michèle was present every step of the way: for the incorporation of the organization, the grant applications, the search for and set up of the space, the meetings with the board of directors, and the organization of fundraising and entertainment events," says Jacinthe Garand, a close

---

41. Interview with Jean-Marc Dupont, July 31, 2019 (my translation).

childhood friend of Michèle's.[42] "We had known each other forever, from before we even went to school together!"[43]

The group is also part of the Cadets Corps 1937 of Lac-Mégantic, which brings together teenagers aged twelve to eighteen. Mimi, as she's nicknamed, joins in 1982 as part of the brass band; she plays the trumpet. She loves music and also plays flute and piano.

The following year, the group of friends travels to Alberta to participate in a student exchange. They stay with local families for ten days, then host the teenagers they visited for ten days. The experience brings the twenty-six participants closer together. In Lac-Mégantic, a city surrounded by nature, this camaraderie is expressed around campfires, or through camping and ice fishing.... Stéphane Therrien can still picture Michèle walking on the lake that shares a name with the city and freezes in the winter.

"With two other people, I had built an ice fishing shack with a small wood stove inside. One day when it was very cold—there was a snowstorm—who did we see arrive on the ice? Michèle, with two friends. I said 'What are you doing? You could have gotten lost on the lake!' She answered 'We just came to say hi and we wanted to make sure you were okay.' She wasn't even fishing, she was just bringing her ray of sun, her smile!"[44]

When Michèle leaves for Montreal in the mid-1980s, it's as hard for her friends as it is for her. Her parents separated a little earlier, and her mother went back to school to study accounting. Now she's found a job that seems most interesting at the Montreal Museum of Fine Arts.

Thérèse Martin leaves with Manon, her youngest. Michèle stays in Lac-Mégantic a few more weeks, long enough to finalize her work at the Maison des Jeunes. She stays with Cécile Martin, her mother's older sister.

Once settled in Montreal, she stays in touch with her friends. This was before the Internet, e-mail, and Facebook. Back then, people still wrote letters, and Michèle writes a lot of them. "We wrote to each other almost every week until the terrible tragedy," says Jean-François Cloutier, another friend.[45]

---

42. Correspondence with Jacinthe Garand, August 6, 2019 (my translation).
43. Interview with Jacinthe Garand, August 1, 2019 (my translation).
44. Interview with Stéphane Therrien, July 30, 2019 (my translation).
45. Interview with Jean-François Cloutier, July 31, 2019.

Michèle on a trip to Baie-James.

Michèle and her mother, Thérèse Martin, whom she was very close to.

Michèle was still deeply attached to her part of the world. She would go once or twice a year to visit family and friends, and she was considering buying a piece of land to have a pied-à-terre in the area. "Mimi would often say: 'I have to come back to Mégantic,'" remembers Stéphane Therrien.

Her extended family remembers her with great affection. She was charming, warm, radiant, and loved life, says her aunt Cécile. And she was extremely gentle. Yes, "whenever she was here, we were all under her spell," she insists.[46]

It was more than her smile. She had a unique *je-ne-sais-quoi* that attracted people. "Her presence was calming," says Jean-Marc.

Michèle was a Cartesian—she would analyze her options in order to find solutions to her problems. She knew how to take calculated risks, says Stéphane. "As early as in high school, we knew that things were going to be different for Michèle, that she was probably going to go in a non-traditional career for women," he adds.

"She was smart, she wanted to pursue her studies in order to make a difference. It was something that would often come up—she wanted to help, to improve things," remembers her aunt.

She eventually chooses engineering and has to work hard to attain her goal—both in pure sciences in cégep and at Polytechnique. "It took a lot of efforts to get there," remarks Jacinthe Garand. But she was happy in the metallurgical engineering program. Very happy, confirms Jean-François.

Especially since she's there with her boyfriend, Stéphane, whom she met in January 1986.

She likes him enough to refuse to introduce him to Lac-Mégantic in the rain. The first time he sees this part of the world she loves so much, she wants it to be at its best. She also likes him enough to follow him on a fishing trip to Baie-James.

Jacinthe, amused, looks at the photo where her friend—so stylish, so feminine, always so well groomed—is posing in her socks with fish and a fishing line. "When I saw this, I thought, 'Wow! She had to be seriously in love!' She really enjoyed that trip."

When Michèle died, she was twenty-one. She was planning on getting engaged in the spring.

46. Interview with Cécile Martin, August 5, 2019.

– ※ –

After December 6

Jacinthe wears the memory of Michèle on her finger. Literally.

"When she was very young, her godmother gave her a child's ring and Michèle immediately lost it. We spent the rest of the day looking for it. And we tried again several times after that. Many years later—Michèle wasn't even in Mégantic anymore—the new owners of the house removed the carpet and found the ring. They managed to give it back to her. So, after her death, when her mother asked me if I wanted a souvenir, that's what I asked for. Since then, it's been on my little finger. It's so small…"

After the tragedy, her friends publish a letter in *L'Écho de Frontenac*, the local weekly paper, to celebrate her perseverance, her enthusiasm, her dreams of peace, and her laugh, which "will forever resonate in the hallways of Polytechnique."[47]

"There's not a day I don't think about her," says Jean-François. For his part, Jean-Marc posts a photo of Michèle on his Facebook page every December 6 as a way to preserve her memory. Friends from that time acknowledge his gesture.

Michèle and her mother, Thérèse, had a very special bond. "A great complicity," says Cécile. In fact, in journalist Francine Pelletier's documentary dedicated to the tragedy, Thérèse says that as soon as she heard the news about the Polytechnique massacre, she knew that her daughter was one of the victims: "I immediately felt that something had happened to Mimi."[48]

Later, Thérèse wrote a letter to her daughter. From the first words, their deep bond is apparent: "Michèle, my daughter, my best friend, I used to tell you my most intimate secrets. In your presence, the Master of Time would stop for a moment, and let me enjoy a few privileged moments with my child."

47. "Nous nous souviendrons de toi, Michèle" [We will remember you, Michèle], *L'Écho de Frontenac*, January 23, 1990 (my translation).
48. Francine Pelletier, "Montreal Massacre: Legacy of Pain," *Fifth Estate*, CBC, December 1, 1999.

To prevent another similar tragedy from happening, and because her daughter abhorred violence ("she had no enemies," Jean-Marc points out), Thérèse will join other relatives of the victims in the Coalition for Gun Control.

"Michèle's death was extremely painful for her sister, Manon, and for Thérèse," confides Cécile. "My sister was a very happy person, who always saw the positive in everything. She continued to laugh, but she would say to me: 'I always have a veil in front of my eyes, a veil of sadness.' And I could see it."

Thérèse died from cancer in 2007. Her pain never went away.

Annie St-Arneault

IN DECEMBER 1989, while Annie St-Arneault is finishing her degree at Polytechnique, a choice presents itself: she can either take a job at the Alcan smelters in Saguenay, where she has interviewed, or she can join her brother Serge, a missionary in Africa, to work on community projects.

She admires her older sibling whose journey she finds inspiring. But she hasn't told him about her project yet, which would allow her to combine humanitarian work with science, one of her dreams. She just mentioned it in passing, in the fall of 1989, to her very best friend, Sonia Beauregard.

These two have been an inseparable duo since they were four years old. It was friendship at first sight while playing in the park, before they even went to kindergarten. A very special connection, like a fusion of two souls. "I've had extraordinary friends, but I've never experienced that again," says Sonia today.[49]

They ran wild together and knew each other by heart. Sonia likes to point out that Annie was curious and thoughtful, and that she always tried to get off the beaten path. As proof, the following anecdote:

Annie and her best friend, Sonia Beauregard.

They're in fifth or sixth grade and all the students have to present a research project of their own to their classmates. One by one, they get up

49. Interview with Sonia Beauregard, June 25, 2019.

and talk about their cat, their dog, their hamster...the subjects are not terribly varied. But Annie keeps hers a mystery. "She came in with something and she didn't want to show it to me. It was a secret, as if she were working for the FBI!"

When her turn comes, what does she present? The horizon! Which she has drawn as a time sequence on transparencies.

"It was a bit like a comic strip in motion. She had drawn a boat on the ocean; we could see the entire sail. On the next drawing, the boat was sailing towards the horizon and the sunset, so it was gradually sinking into the ocean leaving only the mast and the sail. One drawing later, all that was left was the small pirate flag at the very top. And finally, it was all gone. So, it was proof that the Earth is round."

Sonia adds: "It always stuck with me. Every time I go to the ocean and I see a boat, I think about her presentation. And I tell myself, 'You have to give it to her, at ten or eleven, wanting to talk about the horizon when everyone else is talking about hamsters and dogs....'"

Another example among many? This one: Fourth grade. They have to make a clown with rice dyed in different colors.

"Like the other kids, I picked up a chunk of red rice, put glue on it, stuck it on the hat—and the hat was done! But Annie decided to glue the grains of rice one by one. For a week, she spent all her recesses on that. The teacher told her that she didn't have to do the entire clown that way, but she was determined. And when it was done, it was fabulous!"

This detail-oriented young woman is an artist. At a very young age, she's already writing poems. She sends them to her friend, who answers in kind. "But mine weren't the same caliber!" says Sonia.

In high school, they're both members of wind symphonies: the one at school and the one in their city of La Tuque. Through them, they participate in the Festival des Harmonies du Québec, held every year in Sherbrooke. Annie plays transverse flute.

They also do theater with the troupe Les Ouragans. That's when Annie decides to create a show under the theme "What can we do about pollution?" Jean-François Caron, a future writer, gets on board with the project. The play is titled *Les amis des poilus, si on dépolluait*. Annie is deeply

Annie as a teenager in La Tuque.

invested. In cégep as well as in university, she continues to dabble in theater, even creating a play for youth in the summer before her death.

Still, science is what interests her most. And it sets her apart. Not only is she always a step ahead, which makes all of her classmates sigh (What is that question? What is she talking about?), but in high school, she joins the poorly attended Science Club. It comprises eight boys and a single girl: her! Yet, Annie is not there to fight for feminism, which the school principal clumsily congratulates her for, but because she likes it. Period.

Enrolling at Polytechnique is a given for her, just like opting for mechanical engineering. She likes concrete things; she likes building, interacting with the environment. Most of all she's hoping to change it, for the love of people.

"She would take our arm while she was talking to us; she liked touching people. She was a very expressive woman, always in a good mood, always ready to help others, to tell them that she loved them. Truly, a woman with a very big heart," remembers France Chrétien, a classmate and a survivor of the massacre, from which Annie won't return.[50]

"From a very young age, she was an idealist altruist. The Dalai Lama had nothing on her!" says Sonia. She even had a kind of naïveté; for her, there was kindness in everyone, while I would say: 'No, Annie, some people are just plain dangerous.'"

– ※ –

50. Interview with France Chrétien, July 25, 2019.

After December 6

When Sonia received the call telling her that her best friend was dead, she didn't believe it. "I cried, but not a lot. I was convinced that it was a mistake, that it was impossible given the number of people who were at Polytechnique...."

Same denial at the wake at Université de Montréal, and the funeral at the Notre-Dame Basilica. Too big, too many people, too official, too everything.

Sonia turned her back on the tragedy and on her pain for thirty years, not even knowing where her soulmate was buried. It was only in the spring of 2019 that she finally accepted the pain. When she decided to go to her friend's grave for the first time, the St-Arneault family went with her.

It was in July 2019, and it was a very intense moment. The St-Arneaults' generosity, their warm welcome, their kindness, left a strong impression on Sonia. She was reconnecting with Annie again through them, as if she were still living through the members of her family.[51]

She also finally opened the box of souvenirs filled with newspaper articles and some of Annie's belongings that relatives had sent to her over the years. In it, she found a book of poetry written by her friend. Her big brother Serge had it published in September 2011. It contains a collection of poems that Annie wrote between the ages of eleven and twenty-three. It was re-edited in the spring of 2018.

On his personal blog, Serge explains that he wants to honor the memory of his sister: "Her tragic death deprives us of the presence of an exceptional woman. Her poetry reveals a deep and sometimes tormented soul. We hope this book will give her back her voice, which was unfairly stolen from her."[52]

In 2015, La Tuque, where the young woman was born, renamed the municipal library in her honor. It was the first building in the city to bear someone's name. Inside the Annie-St-Arneault Library, a space has been dedicated to her memory.

The municipality insisted on collaborating closely with the family.

51. Correspondence with Sonia Beauregard, September 17, 2019.
52. www.sergestarno.com, accessed on September 7, 2019 (my translation).

"There were several possible options, but it quickly became apparent that the library was the best place, since she loved poetry and had a great thirst for knowledge," explained Normand Beaudoin, Mayor of La Tuque, at the inauguration.[53]

It was a balm for the family, who were devastated by the tragedy. In December 2011, on the occasion of a commemorative ceremony held in La Tuque, Annie's mother, Laurette Perron-St-Arneault, who couldn't attend for health reasons, had someone read the following message: "The Polytechnique tragedy filled me with feelings of fear and emptiness. My daughter's absence was very difficult to overcome and still remains a deep wound whose pain is only alleviated by periods of silence and reflection."[54]

53. Audrey Tremblay, "Annie St-Arneault restera gravée dans l'histoire" [Annie St-Arneault will remain etched in history], *Le Nouvelliste*, September 19, 2015 (my translation).

54. Gabriel Delisle, "La mémoire d'Annie St-Arneault toujours vivante à La Tuque" [The memory of Annie St-Arneault still alive in La Tuque], *Le Nouvelliste*, December 7, 2011 (my translation).

Annie Turcotte

TWENTY-YEAR-OLD ANNIE is a fun-loving person. Even her mailbox proves it.

The young woman from Granby moved to Montreal to pursue her studies at École Polytechnique, like her big brother Donald, who is five years older, did before her.

She shares an apartment with her brother Christian, two years her elder, and also a student. They live in one of the buildings around Université de Montréal. To identify their mailbox, they use not only their two first names, but also a smiley face.[55]

It's not surprising. Their older brother, Donald, talks about that time by quoting Christian: "He used to tell me, 'We would get the giggles.'"[56] Long minutes unable to talk because they were laughing so hard! A family trait that all three of them share.

This cheery nature doesn't prevent the young woman from concentrating on and succeeding in her classes. "She was studying materials engineering and was very concerned with everything that had to do with nature and the environment," says Donald.

55. "Remembering the Polytechnique victims," *Montreal Gazette*, December 5, 2014.
56. Interview with Donald Turcotte, September 16, 2019 (my translation).

Annie and her father, René.

Annie (center) with her friends Nancy, Marie-Josée, and Patricia.

At the same time, she is such a unifier that, in the Turcotte family, no one would have been surprised if she had gone into politics or diplomacy. She likes being surrounded by people and working with them. A bit like her parents who, for a long time, owned a motel with a bar and restaurant in Rigaud, where Annie grew up as a child, and later operated a motel in Granby.

Granby is where Annie spends her teenage years, where she succeeds at everything: she collects As all through high school at Séminaire du Verbe divin, and she's a member of the city's swim club, through which she competes in many meets.

A generous person, she gives free swimming lessons at a summer camp for disabled youth, and does the same with children who stay at the family motel. But no matter what, children flock to her. "Every time we went somewhere, they would all be on top of her! She was incredible with them," says her brother.

Her friends adore her too, and she has lots of them! Especially since she has her own car and doesn't drink. When she goes out with her girlfriends—which she loves doing—she drives everyone home at the end of the night, gently teasing her dad who worries when she comes home too late.

The car is part of the family legend. It was a used car that wasn't in great condition; the gas tank was leaking. No problem. Annie sets out to fix it, as if this is the easiest thing in the world. And she succeeds!

Annie was always willing to face challenges head-on.

Donald remembers biking through Gaspésie with his sixteen-year-old sister. He, at twenty-one, had thoroughly prepared for the trip, which he had been planning with friends for a long time. "Annie was a swimmer; she had never really been on a bike." But her brother's project interests her, so ready or not, she goes! "And she did it! You really had to have guts!"

At the Turcottes, family members rely on each other. Fully. Including on the eve of December 6, when Annie goes to see Donald.

"She was having a hard time in physics and I helped her. Afterwards, I watched her go to her car and I had a feeling of...I was proud of my little sister," he remembers, moved.

Annie intended to continue her engineering studies, no matter how demanding they were. On December 6, she had taken some time to choose her classes for the next semester.

Annie with her
cousin, Daniel
Bergeron.

Because They Were Women

– ✳ –

After December 6

On the night of the tragedy, Donald is in his car. He's going home from work and listening to the radio. He hears that there's a gunman at Polytechnique. That's scary but luckily, he's aware of his sister's schedule, so he know she's not at school…. Except, he doesn't know that the schedule has been changed for the final presentations.

Christian rapidly finds out that the situation is serious. The apartment is so close to Université de Montréal that one of Annie's classmates rushes to it as soon as he can to warn him that a man is shooting women, adding: "I think Annie was hit."

Christian immediately informs the family. Donald joins him to make a round of the hospitals. In vain. They go back to Université de Montréal and, like the other families, they have to wait hours to find out what happened to their sister. The wait nurtures hope.

"We were kidding ourselves, we kept believing. But deep down, we knew Annie: if she had been alive, she would have let us know," says Donald. She never would have wanted her family to worry.

Then it was their turn to be called into the makeshift morgue at Polytechnique. Their Annie was in a body bag. Someone opened it slightly, enough for Donald to recognize his sister. But Christian demanded that the bag be opened in full in order to see the entire body, to be completely sure. Hope until the end….

After the mortuary chapel at Université de Montréal, the Turcotte family chooses to hold a private funeral. It takes place at Église Saint-Luc de Granby. The altar is decorated with Christmas ornaments, as the young woman would have liked, says a friend of the family to *The Gazette*.[57] Some 500 people show up, including students from Polytechnique and from the Séminaire de Granby, where Annie had studied and where classes had been suspended for the occasion. News stories mentioned that the emotion in the room was palpable.

57. Op. cit.

For Annie's parents, mourning took a very long time. Journalist Isabelle Hachey, who met them in 2014 at the 25th anniversary of the tragedy, wrote: "For eight long years, Annie Turcotte's parents didn't touch her bedroom. Her souvenirs, her books, her clothes cleanly folded in her chest of drawers, were ready for the return of a young woman who would never return."[58]

In an interview with *La Voix de l'Est*, Granby's daily newspaper, the couple explained how excruciating the first year was. "We were there physically but that's all," said René Turcotte, Annie's father.[59] Even anger took a long time to rise to the surface so shaken the couple was by what had happened.

"My father had a spark in his eyes, which disappeared after my sister's death. I would even say that his shoulders became rounder," says Donald today.

But they finally come to accept what happened, in part thanks to a note found by Carmen Pépin when she was sorting through her daughter's belongings. Annie had written it when she was seventeen. It said: "I'm not afraid of death, I'm afraid of the pain that surrounds it. I hope to die in some kind of accident, in the middle of the action."[60]

And in a way, that's what happened.

So, the family moved on to the next step: preserving the memory of their beloved child. For example, by getting together every year around March 1, which is Annie's birthday.[61] And by participating in the commemorations of the massacre, so she's not forgotten. Every year, a large white ribbon, the symbol of the Polytechnique tragedy, hangs on their front door.

"It immortalizes our daughters. It also shows that we're not the only ones to condemn violence against women," René explained to *La Voix de l'Est*.[62] He died in 2018.

58. Isabelle Hachey, "Les autres victimes de Marc Lépine" [Marc Lépine's other victims], *La Presse*, December 1, 2014 (my translation).

59. Karine Blanchard, "Leur fille parmi les victimes de Marc Lépine: 'On a appris à vivre avec le décès d'Annie'" [Their daughter among Marc Lépine's victims: 'We learned to live with Annie's death], *La Voix de l'Est*, December 6, 2014.

60. Isabelle Hachey, op. cit. (my translation).

61. "En souvenir d'elles" [In their memory], *La Presse*, op. cit.

62. Karine Blanchard, op. cit.

Acknowledgments

MOST BOOKS ARE WRITTEN from within a deep sense of solitude. As writers, why do we want to add our words to everything that already exists? Work when no one is asking us for anything?

But sometimes we write knowing that we're surrounded. That we're just a hand moving the text forward, while words and emotions float around, ready to be caught and aligned on the page so they can be shared.

I lived this rare experience while being fully aware that I owe it to the generosity of people who were on the frontline of the Polytechnique tragedy.

For them, going back thirty years wasn't a given—it was painful and upsetting. Some of them thought for a long time before they answered the invitation extended to them. "You really stirred me," said one person. "Thirty years...that's longer than she lived," a friend who was approached to talk about one of the victims suddenly realized. "Maybe it's time I open up," concluded another who hesitated for a long time.

My first thanks must go to them.

Thank you for the trust extended to me by families, friends, former Polytechnique students, and the personnel of the institution.

Thank you for the memories, thank you for the words, thank you for the tears. Thank you for invading my head and my heart while I was writing this book.

– ※ –

The idea for this book comes from the Comité Mémoire, in charge, for the last several years, of the December 6 commemorative ceremony on Mount Royal. Two people approached me to be the author: Jacques Duchesneau, member of the committee, and Pierre Cayouette, editor-in-chief at Éditions La Presse.

I met the former through my journalistic work, and I know the latter very well. In fact, I've known him for thirty years—when I started as a journalist at *Le Devoir* at the end of November 1989, he was one of the bosses. On December 6 that same year, I was assigned to cover the unimaginable story unfolding at École Polytechnique, and Pierre was my bureau chief.

While some editing executives showed reservations about my lack of experience—and the fact that I was a feminist—Pierre's trust in me was total. Yet I have never thanked him. So, I was certainly not going to refuse the invitation he was extending to me thirty years later, to dive back into this tragedy that marked both his and my early career. I saw that his trust in me hasn't wavered.

Jacques Duchesneau offered a lot more than his support. He's offered his friendship. He believed in my idea to locate the Polytechnique tragedy within a broader frame, to insert the story of that horrible night into a history of women begun decades earlier, and that is still unfolding today. And he did everything to make my job easy.

Day after day—including on weekends—I've been able to count on a remarkable young woman named Annie-Clara Gravel. As a member of the Comité Mémoire, she was a bridge between relatives of the victims and everything about this project, and masterfully conducted very delicate interviews. I so often called on her that she was like a shadow over my shoulder, helping me stay the course.

I also owe quality interviews to Lyne Dunberry. In addition, she thoroughly verified the thousands of details spread out over five decades included in this book. Her work really impressed me. Similarly, the knowledge and memories of André Tessier, responsible of the police operation during the tragedy, proved precious.

I was equally impressed by the efficiency of Florence Scanvic from the Communications and Public Relations Services at Polytechnique, and member of the Comité Mémoire, who was able to locate people who were themselves surprised by it. (As one interviewee cheerfully exclaimed: "How in the world did you manage to get to me?!") And I also need to mention the speed with which Claire Bertin transcribed a whole lot of interviews in a very short amount of time. "Here, done!" Oh, wow!

Thank you also to Catherine Bergeron, president of the Comité Mémoire, for showing me warmth and kindness beyond the simple overseeing of a project she felt strongly about.

Thank you to the other members of the committee, who join the four mentioned above. Michel Petit, Romain A. Gayet, Jonathan Landry-Leclerc, Jim Edward, and Martine Robert worked hard to make this book happen and observe the 30th anniversary of a tragedy we can't forget with dignity.

I also have to thank Pascal Genêt, of Éditions La Presse, for his patience and his understanding in the face of the scope of the work, and the production deadlines that had to be adjusted as a result of it.

And Nathalie Provost, who met with me for a long time in June when I was getting lost in the multiple perspectives and I needed to talk freely, without adhering to a structure. She's a Polytechnique survivor; I covered the event. We could think together. She was a superb interlocutor.

A special thank you to my daughter, Myriam Boileau, my twenty-year-old test reader. This book had to evoke something tangible for today's youth. She had no problem playing the role of first reader, and that really helped me.

Finally, a huge thank you to André Lacroix, my precious spouse. Only he knows how much this going back in time consumed me, upsetting my schedule, and occupying all my thoughts. How much I didn't want to betray this wonderful project and the people who believed in it. Whenever I felt overwhelmed (Is this the right angle? The right tone? Did I forget anyone?), he would calmly say that I would find my way back. It's good to know that someone is waiting for you there.

All these thanks don't prevent me from taking final responsibility for the content of this book. Any mistake, imprecision, or omission that you may find are mine. And I remain extremely proud to see my name attached to this duty of memory.

PHOTO CREDITS

LIST OF ACRONYMS AND ABBREVIATIONS

AEP - Association des étudiants de Polytechnique, now Association étudiante de Polytechnique

CAQ - Coalition Avenir Québec

CBC - Canadian Broadcasting Corporation

CÉGEP - Collège d'enseignement général et professionnel

CEQ - Corporation des enseignants du Québec until 1974 when it becomes Centrale de l'enseignement du Québec, and then Centrale des syndicats du Québec (CSQ) in 2000

CFAC - Canadian Firearms Advisory Committee

CLSC - Centres locaux de services communautaires

CSN - Confédération des syndicats nationaux

DEC - Diplôme d'études collégiales

ETS - École de technologie supérieure

FFQ - Fédération des femmes du Québec

FLF - Front de libération des femmes du Québec

FPJQ - Fédération professionnelle des journalistes du Québec

FTQ - Fédération des travailleurs et travailleuses du Québec

ISQ - Institut de la statistique du Québec

LVR - *La Vie en rose*

RQCALACS - Regroupement québécois des centres d'aide et de lutte contre les agressions à caractère sexuel

MP - Member of Parliament

MUC Police - Montreal Urban Community Police Service

NFB - National Film Board of Canada

OIQ - Ordre des ingénieurs du Québec

PTSD - Post-traumatic stress disorder

RCMP - Royal Canadian Mounted Police

SPCUM - Service de police de la Communauté urbaine de Montréal (Montreal Urban Community Police Service). It later became the City of Montreal Police Service

UN - United Nations

UQAM - Université du Québec à Montréal

THE FEMINIST HISTORY SOCIETY SERIES

The Feminist History Society is committed to creating a lasting record of the women's movement in Canada and Québec for the fifty years between 1960 and the year of the Society's founding, 2010. Feminism has a history that predates the 1960s and continues long after 2010.

The energy that women brought to their quest for equality in these decades is beyond dispute, and it is that energy that we capture in this series. Our movement is not over and new campaigns are upon us. But the FHS series presents an opportunity to take stock of the wide-ranging campaigns for equality that occurred in Canada between 1960 and 2010. There was much transformative social, economic, civil, political, and cultural change.

We maintain an open call for submissions (https://secondstorypress.ca/submissions/) across a full range of approaches to the period, including autobiographies, biographies, edited collections, pictorial histories, plays and novels. There will be many different authors as all individuals and organizations that were participants in the movement are encouraged to contribute. We make every effort to be inclusive of gender, race, class, geography, culture, dis/ability, language, sexual identity, and age.

Beth Atcheson, Constance Backhouse, Lorraine Greaves, Diana Majury, and Beth Symes form the working collective of the Feminist History Society. Margie Wolfe, Publisher, Second Story Feminist Press Inc. and her talented team of women, are presenting the Series.

https://secondstorypress.ca/feminist-history-society-series/